Initiatives with Youth-at-risk in Hong Kong

Initiatives with Youth-at-risk in Hong Kong

Edited by
Francis Wing-lin LEE

City University of Hong Kong Press

First published 2009

ISBN: 978-962-937-174-6

Published by
City University of Hong Kong Press
Tat Chee Avenue
Kowloon, Hong Kong
Website: www.cityu.edu.hk/upress
E-mail: upress@cityu.edu.hk

Printed in Hong Kong

To Professor Sammy Wai-sang CHIU

My best friend

Contents

Foreword

I am honoured to be invited to write a brief foreword to this important publication: *Initiatives with Youth-at-risk in Hong Kong*.

After 35 years as a front-line youth worker, and subsequently a policy researcher and advisor to the Hong Kong SAR Government, I am convinced that "youth-at-risk" is an important population that can become a valuable asset to the Hong Kong community at large—given the appropriate support, guidance, training, and space for participation and contribution.

This book has successfully gathered some creative and groundbreaking initiatives in the arena of services for the youth-at-risk. The outreaching approach has enabled youth workers to interact with young people who are not comfortable with the traditional centre-based approach to youth services. The Community Support Service Scheme has contributed significantly towards building up the social capital for the young people in the community.

The Police School Liaison Scheme is a successful example of cross-discipline collaboration between social workers, teachers, and the police officers. The Hotline Service is an important platform for preventive, and restorative services for youth-at-risk.

The Adventure Counselling Programme has proven to be a successful form of experiential learning for the youth-at-risk. The youth in social withdrawal presents a new challenge to youth workers: we are rethinking new channels of reaching this hidden population, and new ways of engaging them in social participation. I am impressed with the recent initiatives in Restorative Justice Approach, which have proven to be effective modes of service especially for deviant juveniles.

Since the launching of the "Understanding Adolescents Project" in the primary and secondary schools as a model of preventive services for adolescents potentially at risk, I had multiple opportunities of interaction with youth workers from different countries of the world. I find this kind of international and cross-cultural exchange very profitable and eye opening. It is my sincere wish that this informative and thought-provoking book can be a further step in increasing the awareness of the strategic importance of reaching the youth-at-risk in the community—not only in Hong Kong , but also in other cities of the global village.

Finally, I wish to express my warmest appreciation to Dr. Francis Wing-lin Lee for his vision and passion for services targeted at youth-at-risk; and my sincere gratitude to the youth workers and agencies for their courage and insight demonstrated by the creative initiatives of working with youth-at-risk in Hong Kong. I am proud to be part of this dynamic community of youth workers in Hong Kong.

Philemon Yuen-wan CHOI
Hon. General Secretary
Breakthrough
(Ex-chairperson of Commission on Youth, HKSAR)

Preface

After the book *Working with Youth-at-Risk in Hong Kong* was published in 2005, there have been sayings that more books on introducing different initiatives of working with at-risk youth in Hong Kong should be published so that different kinds of local services for this target population can be known. It is primarily with this aim that the present book is edited. It has been mentioned that since young people are usually being perceived as immature, having low self-esteem, lack of coping ability and self-control, they are usually regarded as more at-risk (Lee, 2005). The definition of "at-risk" provided by McWhirter *et al.* (1998) has provided a comprehensible one. As stated, they defined "at-risk" as:

> *"A set of presumed cause-and-effect dynamics that place the child or adolescent in danger of negative future events...a situation that is not necessarily current but that can be anticipated in the absence of intervention." (p. 7)*

So appropriate early interventions are needed for young people who exhibit certain kinds of deviant behaviour otherwise the consequences (effects) would be problematic. With reference to the at-risk continuum of young people they proposed (McWhirter *et al.*, 1998:7–9), they supported the ideas of prevention and early intervention of youth-at-risk (YAR) of different socio-economic profiles (McWhirter *et al.*, 1998).

The present book will put emphasis on both theoretical and practical parts on the different services and work with YAR in Hong Kong. With reference to the exhibited "problems" of the young people at different time, there are different approaches and services to the YAR in the territory. This book tries to introduce some well heard and current ones to the readers. The intended audience of this book is basically those who want to know more about the theoretical as well as the practical sides of the work with YAR of different exhibited "problems" (e.g., social workers, teachers, university and college students, etc.). This could also be a text book or a reference in courses on youth work in the universities and colleges.

It is a bit disappointed to say that most of the initiatives for YAR introduced in this text are reactive instead of proactive, that is, their establishment and existence are in response to the occurrence of certain kinds of YAR behaviour or phenomena. Among the eight initiatives to be introduced in this book, only the Police School Liaison Scheme could be regarded as proactive and early intervention programmes for the YAR. The other seven initiatives to be introduced include (1) District Youth Outreaching Social Work Team, (2) Overnight Outreaching Service for Young Night Drifters, (3) Community Support Service Scheme, (4) Hotline Service for Youth-at-Risk, (5) Counselling Centre for Young Psychotropic Substance Abusers, (6) Adventure Counselling Programme for Female Substance Abusers and (7) Working with Youth with Social Withdrawal. They could be regarded as reactive services to different "problems" of the YAR.

The Police School Liaison Scheme already has its existence since 1974 as part of the community policing strategy. In August 2001, as part of a comprehensive programme of support services for YAR, 33 Secondary School Liaison Officer (SSLO) posts at Sergeant rank were created to strengthen police commitment in juvenile crime prevention work. It is believed that "to reduce young people's inclination to seek recognition and support from gangs, preventive programmes should focus on early identification of and intervention for potential-at-risk youth." (www.info.gov.hk/police/hkp-home/english/pprb/schlia/slossloprg.htm). Through some service reorganisations, in September 2002, 16 District Youth Outreaching Social Work Teams (YOTs) run by 11 Non-governmental Organizations (NGOs) were established in 16 priority communities in the territories to deliver services to street gangs in the communities. Attached to 18 Integrated Children and Youth Services Centres (ICYSCs) in the territory, Overnight Outreaching Service for Young Night Drifters (YNDs) in the form of 18 teams for the whole territory was initiated in September 2001. Two teams of Community Support Service Scheme (CSSS) are run by the Social Welfare Department of the Government and 5 CSSSs are run by NGOs. The CSSSs run by NGOs are also attached to ICYSCs and mainly deliver guidance service to police cautioned young people (www.swd.gov.hk/en/index/site pubsvc/page_young). The Hong Kong Federation of Youth Groups (an NGO) has received subvention from the Government since 1995 to run hotline service for YAR. With its convenient, private and immediate counselling services, the Service has proved to be an effective one in helping YAR in crisis situation (www.swd.gov.hk/en/ index/ site_pubsvc/page_ young). Five centres for psychotropic substance abusers run by NGOs are now in operation. This book will introduce their services for young substance abusers. Both theoretical and practical accounts will be mentioned. Adventure-based Counselling (ABC) programmes for boosting the self-esteem, confidence and social skills of YAR have been widely employed in working with YAR (or young people in general) in the recent decade. How effective these intervention programmes are for substance abusers? Youth with social withdrawal symptoms recently have drawn much media coverage and public attention. With professional consultation with and support from an academic in the Social Work Department of the Hong Kong Baptist University, the Hong Kong Christian Service (an NGO) has initiated counselling services for this kind of YAR. The related chapter might give us an answer.

How are we going to assess the effectiveness of these intervention programmes? We have invited academics, frontline practitioners and supervisors of related services with relevant expertise as contributors to address to the issues.

At the end of this book, there is a chapter on "Restorative Justice Approach to Youth-at-risk". Although this approach has been promoted for several decades and widely adopted in some western countries, e.g. the U.S., U.K., New Zealand, and Australia, for disposing young offenders (Bazemore, 1998; Johnstone, 2002, 2003 & 2004; Lo *et al.*, 2005; Maxwell *et al.*, 2000; Morris and Young, 2000; Sullivan and Tifft, 2001), it's application to YAR has just been recently promoted in Hong Kong. With the energetic support and enthusiasm of a group of school principals, social workers, and academics, the Centre for Restoration of Human Relationships was established in August 2000 (Wong, 2005). Through the programmes and services of this Centre, the practice of Restorative Justice (RJ) for YAR in local context has been energetically promoted (www.restoration.com.hk). With the declining faith in the retributive and rehabilitative approaches to deviance, the RJ model has gained its popularity as a preferred alternative, especially for deviant juveniles. This approach is introduced so that readers might have an alternative for handling YAR. It is hoped that this book can help readers to be more familiarised with different initiatives in the local context for working with YAR both theoretically and practically.

References

Bazemore, G. (1998). Restorative Justice and Earned Redemption. *American Behavioral Scientist.* Vol. 41(6):768–807.

Johnstone, G. (2002). *Restorative Justice: Ideas, Values, Debates.* London: Willan.

Johnstone, G. (ed.) (2003). *A Restorative Justice Reader: Texts, Sources and Context.* London: Willan.

Johnstone, G. (2004). "Informal and Restorative Justice," in Muncie, J. and Wilson, D. (eds.) *The Cavendish Handbook of Criminal Justice and Criminology.* London: Cavendish.

Lee, F. W. L. (ed.) (2005). *Working with Youth-at-risk in Hong Kong.* Hong Kong: HKU Press.

Lo, T. W., Wong, D. and Maxwell, G. (2005). *Alternatives to Prosecution: Rehabilitative and Restorative Models of Youth Justice.* Singapore: Marshall Cavendish Academic.

Maxwell, G., Morris, A. and van Ness, D. (2000). "Introducing Restorative Justice," in Maxwell, G. and Morris, A. (eds.) *Restorative Justice for Juveniles: Conferencing, Mediation and Circle.* New York: Hart Publishing, pp. 3–16.

McWhirter, J. J., McWhirter, B. T., McWhirter, A. M. and McWhirter, E. H. (1998). *At-Risk Youth: A Comprehensive Responses.* (2nd edition) N. Y.: Brooks/Cole Publishing Company.

Morris, A. and Young, W. (2000). "Reforming Criminal Justice: The potential of Restorative Justice," in Strang, H. and Braithwaite, J. (eds.) *Restorative Justice: Philosophy to Practice.* Aldershot: Ashgate, pp. 11–31.

Sullivan, D. and Tifft, L. (2001). *Restorative Justice: Healing the Foundations of Our Everyday Lives.* New York: Willow Tree Press.

Wong, D. S. W. (March 2005). "Restorative Justice for Juveniles in Hong Kong: Reflections of a Practitioner," (Plenary) *Proceedings of the Sixth International*

Conference on Conferencing, Circles and Other Restorative Practices. Penrith, Australia: International Institute of Restorative Practices, pp. 71–85.

Websites

www.restoration.com.hk

www.swd.gov.hk/en/index/site_pubsvc/page_young

www.info.gov.hk/police/hkp-home/english/pprb/schlia/slossloprg.htm

Acknowledgements

The completion of this book project owes much to the support of many people.

First of all, I would like to thank all the contributors in this book, as it is their contributions that make this book possible. I would also like to express my gratitude to Dr. Philemon Yuen-wan Choi who wrote the Foreword for this volume. It is his concern for the "youth-at-risk" that inspires my idea of editing this book. I would also like to express my deepest thanks to Professor Sammy Chiu, who gives his unconditional support to me spiritually all the way in my life course. This book is dedicated to him.

List of Contributors

CHAN Kwok-kai, Benson	Social Worker Cheer Lutheran Centre Hong Kong Lutheran Social Service
CHAN Wai-leung, Charlie	Social Work Officer Youth and Community Service Caritas-Hong Kong [Supervisor of Caritas District Youth Outreaching Social Work Team-Aberdeen]
CHOI Yuen-wan, Philemon	Director Breakthrough Limited [Ex-chairperson of Commission on Youth, HKSAR]
CHOW Chi-man	Project Officer Kowloon East Youth Night Drifters Service Team Assistant Supervisor Kwun Tong District Youth Outreaching Social Service Team Boys and Girls Clubs' Association of Hong Kong
HO Wun-tsz	Teacher Barnabas Charitable Service Association Volunteer Christian Adventurer Counselling Ministry Breakthrough Limited

HSU Siu-man	Supervisor Youth Counselling Centre Hong Kong Federation of Youth Groups
LEE Koon-mei	Service Coordinator Methodist Centre, Hong Kong [Supervisor of Project Phoenix—Community Support Service Scheme]
LEE Tak-shing, Alex	Chief Training Officer Renewal Pavilion Breakthrough Limited
LEE Wing-lin, Francis	Associate Professor Department of Social Work and Social Administration The University of Hong Kong
LO Ming-lai, Daisy	Registered Social Worker Ex-Case Worker Barnabas Charitable Service Association
NG Kwok-hung, Kennedy	Registered Social Worker Stewards Limited Training Director Challenge Course Association
TO Siu-ming	Instructor Hong Kong Institute of Educational Research The Chinese University of Hong Kong [Ex-Social Worker of Cheer Lutheran Centre of Hong Kong Lutheran Social Service]

WONG Cheong-wing, Victor Professor
Department of Social Work
Hong Kong Baptist University

WONG King-har, Fanny Programme Coordinator
Renewal Pavilion
Breakthrough Limited

YUNG Kin-lam, Gary Service Coordinator
Methodist Centre, Hong Kong
[Sai Wan Ho Integrated Children and Youth Services]
[Ex-supervisor of Project Phoenix—Community Support Service Scheme]

List of Illustrations

Figures

Acronyms and Abbreviations

Acronyms	Name in full	Appear First on Page
ABC	Adventure-Base Counselling	103
AC	Adventure Counselling	103
CBA	Cognitive-Behavioural Approach	107
CCPSAs	Counselling Centres for Psychotropic Substance Abusers	81
CID	Criminal Investigation Department	64
CIT	Crisis Intervention Theory	38
CRDA	Central Registry of Drug Abuse	100
CSD	Correctional Services Department	101
CSSS	Community Support Service Scheme	34
CT	Cognitive Therapy	107
CUHK	Chinese University of Hong Kong	19
DATS	District School Support Team	65
DCMM	Diversified Case Management Model	42
DD	Dangerous Drugs	65
DH	Department of Health	101
ELCHK	Evangelical Lutheran Church of Hong Kong	151
FC	Family Conference	49
FGC	Family Group Conferencing	151
FSA	Funding and Service Agreement	21
HA	Hospital Authority	101
HKCS	Hong Kong Christian Service	101

HKFYG	Hong Kong Federation of Youth Groups	73
HKLSS	Hong Kong Lutheran Social Service	81
HKSWU	Hong Kong Social Worker Union	5
ICYSCs	Integrated Children and Youth Service Centres	3
IT	Integrated Team	3
NEET	Not in Education, Employment or Training	130
NGOs	Non-Governmental Organisations	4
OSW	Outreaching Social Work	2
PP	Project Phoenix	34
PPRB	Police Public Relations Bureau	61
PSDS	Police Superintendent's Discretion Scheme	34
PSLS	Police School Liaison Scheme	60
RJ	Restorative Justice	148
SARDA	Society for the Aid and Rehabilitation of Drug Abusers	101
SLOs	School Liaison Officers	60
SSLO	Secondary School Liaison Officer	60
SWD	Social Welfare Department	18
UAP	Understanding the Adolescent Project	103
VOM	Victim-Offender Mediation	53
YAR	Youth-At-Risk	34
YJC	Youth Justice Conferencing	53
YMTs	Youth Mobile Teams	19
YNDs	Young Night-Drifters	10
YO	Youth Outreach	19
YOTs	Youth Outreaching Teams	6

Caring for Youth Series

Edited by:
Francis Wing-lin LEE

Initiatives with Youth-at-risk in Hong Kong

1 DISTRICT YOUTH OUTREACHING SOCIAL WORK TEAM

Charlie Wai-leung CHAN

Introduction

In designing outreaching social work (OSW) service for young people, we need to examine the core value of outreaching social work and to analyse the environment. Without considering these, we may lose the core value and mission of outreaching social work/outreach social work in this ever-changing society. In this chapter, I will firstly describe the difficulties of the development of outreach social work in the past few years, then I will share the challenges and difficulties that we have faced, and finally the way we can go forward.

Blooming Days

Outreach social work for young people in Hong Kong was established in 1979 after the *White Paper on Personal Social Work among Young People in Hong Kong* was published in 1978. The service is designed to reach out and establish contact with young people who may be socially undesirable, delinquent, or self-destructive. The aim is to enhance the social functioning of individual young persons through remedial, preventive and developmental measures (HKCSS, 1983). However, the public, especially from the government, often questioned the service. Lo (1990) said that the government was not satisfied with the performance of outreaching social work, e.g. the caseload was always below standard. Thus, Ng and Man (1985) were commissioned to conduct an evaluation of the service in 1981. The report was completed in 1985 and it confirmed that "youths in the outreaching program were, in general, curbed from further deteriorated in their behaviour problem." (Ng and Man, 1985:219) Through negotiation and the joint efforts of various outreach social work teams, the government finally recognized the work of outreach social work and allowed the service to continue and expand.

Kwok (1999) stated that, from 1987 onwards, outreach social work service entered its golden years. The service was expanded rapidly and outreach social work teams were increased to 34 in 2000, covering the whole territory. In between these two decades, the outreach social workers developed various social work intervention models or strategies to handle various youth problems, such as the application of various theories and therapies, e.g. social learning theory and narrative therapy. The teams also conducted a variety of research to explore youth problems and increase public awareness about various youth problems such as drug abuse, school dropouts and gang issues. All of these eventually helped the outreach social work service to develop a good public image in society. The outreach service represents expertise in working with youth-at-risk. Their tremendous output also reflects the great energy and liveliness of the service.

Gloomy Days

However, the *Report on Review of Children and Youth Centre Services* in 1994 stated that centre services should be improved and a new model, namely integrated approach, should be adopted, i.e. the children and youth centre services should include centre-based service, school social service and the outreach service. Children and young people can get one-stop service from the centres. The service can flexibly deploy their resources and adopt working approaches to meet the multifarious needs of young people in the communities served, and can be responsive to community need. An evaluation conducted by the City University of Hong Kong from 1995 to 1997 confirmed the effectiveness of the integrated team (IT) model, and with approval from the Social Welfare Department, integrated teams were formed to replace children and youth centre services (SWD, 1998:50). Hence, the integrated team model would become the future development of children and youth services, and the IT is renamed as Integrated Children and Youth Service Centre (ICYSC).

ICYSC is regarded as a rising star in the children and youth services in Hong Kong, though there are still many discussions and debates concerning its application (Chan, 1996; Lee, 2002), but as a whole, the field welcomes the proposed model. The government then encouraged the non-governmental organisations (NGOs) to redeploy their own children and youth services as ITs in various districts, but without adding additional resources. Since the integrated model was to be the main development trend in the future, NGOs began to rearrange their own children and youth services to form ITs. The outreach social work teams for young people would become one of the services in ITs. As a result, the number of OSW teams shrank quickly. At the worst moment, only 25 teams were operating and 19 of them had not more than five workers. This exercise has torn OSW teams to pieces (Kwok, 1999). Worse than that, the Social Welfare Department requested that once an ICYSC is formed, the original OSW team should cease serving the area. This is the announcement of the death of the service.

Crisis Vs. Chance

Whenever there is a crisis, there is an opportunity. The establishment of ICYSCs meant that OSW would be replaced by them. Initially, many people thought that ICYSCs would be better. The outreach social work service in an ICYSC would have more manpower because a team with similar manpower would serve only 12,000 of the youth population, while an OSW team would have to serve a population of 100,000 before integration. The ICYSC would also adopt a holistic and total-person approach to serve the clientele, but the original OSW service would only be a remedial service, and finally the integration of school, outreach and centre-based service would allow flexibility in deploying manpower among these three services.

Discrepancies however often occur between theory and practice. The outreach social service in an ICYSC cannot have the above-stated advantages, but rather it is easily neglected and absorbed in practice. The Devil hides behind the application—limited manpower, but greater demand from the community. Most of the outreach workers in an ICYSC need to assume more duties and roles than previously, and thus, they can no longer focus on their clients, i.e. youth-at-risk or gang members.

In 2001, a research conducted by the Hong Kong Social Worker Union (HKSWU) reflected the situation. Outreach social workers in ICYSCs could spend only half of their time in dealing with the street youth. More than 53% of the social workers in ICYSCs reported that the service could only deal with a limited number of street youth, while nearly 70% reported that the outreaching service provided by the ICYSCs was worse than before. In 2002, Lee conducted similar research, finding that the difficulties that outreach workers in ICYSCs encountered included "service target lacked motivation, worker lacked related skills and not enough service delivery time."

These reports reflect most of the reality. The fatal problem in ICYSCs is that the outreach worker, unlike in the past, cannot work in the spots and keep regular contact with the street youth wholeheartedly. Since there are great demands from the community, especially from the school systems, an outreach worker in an ICYSC often will be the first to assist in these works. But much more unfortunately, the outreach clients are the most powerless ones, as they would not voice their needs or even show resistance when they feel they are being labelled as deviants. In these circumstances, their needs will often be neglected when other community members show more readiness to request services from the ICYSC. As a result, even when the workers have good intentions, limited time can be spent on outreach work (HKSWU, 2001).

This situation urges the re-establishment of independent OSW teams which are mainly targeted to work with street youth. A group of outreach workers formed a concern group and met different parties to voice the needs of street youth. The government then showed a positive response and asked the concerned group to submit a proposal. In 2002, the Social Welfare Department finally agreed to set up 16 district youth outreaching teams (YOTs) in Hong Kong to cater the needs of street youth.

Core Elements of Outreaching Social Work

Relationship Building

The gloomy days of the last few years have provided a good opportunity for workers in the service to review the core elements of the service. This review helps workers to understand why OSW is worth maintaining, and even that ICYSCs should be the main trend in development.

According to the *Operational Manual for Outreaching Social Workers* (HKCSS, 1983), the working approach of outreaching is to "work with young people in their natural environment" and to "adopt a systematic helping approach" to assess the needs and problems of young people. This depicts a core element of OSW, i.e. working with young people in their natural environment. As we know, the clients are young people who are detached from the conventional and formal systems, and the characteristics of these young people are that they are unwilling or unmotivated to seek services because they do not feel they need to change their lifestyles. Thus, the worker is required to work in their living environment to understand and develop a mutual dialogue to achieve a fusion of horizon, otherwise resistance may happen (Lee, 1996). In this aspect, the outreach worker needs to spend tremendous time in working in the natural environment and in conducting genuine dialogues with street youth. These work can help workers in connecting with these detached youth and also in understanding them, and thus reducing their resistance and increasing their motivation to be assisted. Through this investment, workers can build up a trusting relationship with the youth, which is of utmost importance for effective intervention (Lee, 1997).

Working with Individuals in Groups

The second core element is to adopt a "case in group" approach in working with the natural gang. The *Operational Manual* (HKCSS, 1983) defined the work approach of OSW as a group work approach. The stages include field observation, rapport building, social relationship, working relationship and termination. Lee (1997) further elaborated the group work approach in an outreaching setting as comprising three elements: "rapport building" (R), "group focus" (G) and "case in group" (C). Lee (1997) considered the ability of workers to build relationships with the natural groups of youth-at-risk to be a crucial aspect in effective/ineffective intervention. After building up a trusting relationship with the group, the worker will often design some tailor-made programmes or services for the group. This will require the worker to be sensitive to the needs and interest of the group, as well as sufficient community resources to support such kinds of programmes. This is extremely important in the present day. Nowadays, outreach workers use various types of programmes, such as training bands, hip hop dancing, beauty courses, war games, etc., to attract the targeted street youth to participate in their programmes. Through their participation, more understanding of their needs can be acquired. Finally, when the relationship between group members and an outreach worker is stable, the outreach worker will try to use individual work or the casework approach to help the targeted youth. This process often lasts one to three years (Lee, 1997).

To allow outreach work with youth-at-risk to be effective, the work within the environment, and the aforementioned core elements should be attended to. Allowing workers to work in the community, allowing sufficient time for them to build up trusting relationship with the clients, the development of dialogues with them, and finally soliciting sufficient community support are all important.

Life after Death: Difficulties Ahead

The setting up of District Youth Outreaching Teams (YOTs) is not the end of the story. It represents a new page of challenges and difficulties for the outreach service. The work is in fact the same as that of the earlier OSW, and YOTs are formed to serve identified at-risk youth and street gangs in 16 prioritised communities in the territory. Though the work is similar, the environment is different.

Each YOT maintains ten professional staff, although the area served and the population is much larger than ever. For example, one team needs to serve Tseung Kwan O and Wong Tai Sin which, in the past, was served by three OSW teams. A larger area served created a lot of administration difficulties. For example, an outreach worker may spend increased time in transportation from one spot to another. The facilities, like interviewing rooms and group activities rooms, are not sufficient. Some YOTs must borrow interviewing rooms from nearby organisations. The inadequate manpower and insufficient resources, in contrast to the huge serving boundaries, force a YOT to set up priority areas to serve and some areas need to put aside.

With the ICYSCs continuing their outreach work in their own serving areas, this creates the question of overlapping of services, and the separation of the work focus between a YOT and an ICYSC is difficult. In a cooperative meeting organised by HKSWU (2002), it was established that, since each ICYSC has its own service direction and priorities in working with street youth, it would be difficult to coordinate the work in the community. Some may ask for more cooperation from the YOT, but others may not. Some may spend more time on street work, while others may not, some may have very strict definition on street youth, while others may not. Nonetheless, the YOT is expected to coordinate and cooperate with most of them. A worker said that, in his working area, there are more than 10 ICYSCs (HKSWU 2002). In another cooperative session among YOTs in 2005, the cooperation between ICYSCs and YOTs still remained at the talking level, and also concerned the overlapping of services, but not the development of more effective coordination and comprehensive services for youth-at-risk between the two services.

The definition of youth-at-risk is confused among the services. Ng and Man (1985) suggested that the OSW should aim at preventing youth from falling into delinquency and crime. The focus should be "unattached youth," i.e. those youth who are not attached to the conventional or normal systems, such as school and family. The *Operational Manual for Outreaching Social Workers* (HKCSS, 1983) has a similar description, but with greater detail. It includes "members of natural gang or street gang;" "unattached young people who are often found loitering without companions;" those who have "poor ties with their families and may run away;" and "school dropouts or potential school dropouts." These descriptions are attempting to use behaviours as indicators to define who should be approached by the outreach social workers, and they are young people loiter in the community with unruly behaviour and poor ties with the conventional systems. As concluded by Chui (2001), "unattached youth" in the Hong Kong context are "those who are more crime-prone but have not yet committed crime." Using this guideline, in the past the outreach worker could often differentiate their work focus from other services. However, with the establishment of ICYSCs, this guideline needs to be revised, since the outreach sub-teams of the ICYSCs will also approach similar targets in the communities served, which will lead to an overlapping of services. Though HKSWU (2001) suggested a continuum to classify what type of youth-at-risk should be approached by YOTs and what type should be the target of ICYSCs, there are still many blurred areas. It suggested that youth in general and groups with deviant youth should be the focus of ICYSCs, and that juvenile gangs should be the focus of YOTs. However, it is very difficult to differentiate whether a group is a group of deviant youth or a juvenile gang. For example, in a group of young people who congregate on a football pitch, some are triad members, while some are still students but have some deviant behaviours, like shop-lifting. Who should be responsible for this gang or group? Is this a gang or only a youth group with deviant behaviour? Is shop-lifting minor deviant behaviour or not? It seems that it is quite difficult to classify the targets only by behavioural terms. Therefore, some teams use geography to classify their work focus, some use age, and some hold regular case conferences. Nonetheless, the problems continue without proper handling.

From 2000 onwards, there are many newly developed services and projects that also target youth-at-risk and that lead to greater competition. The OSW service for young night-drifters (YNDs) (which will be discussed further in the next chapter) is a service which is closely related to YOTs. Since the YNDs also hang around locations similar to those of the clients of YOTs, but at night time (say, from 10:00p.m. to 6:00a.m.), the YNDs most often mix with clients who are already under YOT service. Thus, some youth workers have suggested combining the YOT with the outreach team for YNDs (Chan, 2003). At the time of writing this chapter, the Counselling Centres for Psychotropic Substance Abusers have also been requested to deliver outreach work to young substance abusers in various spots. Lee (2005) lists more than 9 services which are either wholly or partially working with youth-at-risk. In addition to the subvented youth service, many project-based services also aim at doing outreach work with the youth-at-risk, such as the Snow Ball of Hong Kong Federation of Youth Groups and Playsafe Healthy Life Project of Caritas-Hong Kong for young disco-goers. These projects often cooperate with some other NGOs and sectors, such as the medical sectors, police or local organisations. These newly developed services create a new work environment for YOTs. How to redefine the roles and functions of YOTs is an issue to be dealt with in the near future.

The Way Forward

In this highly complicated environment, how can the YOTs develop new programmes for street youth? Spergel (1995) has examined several outreach programmes and has found that some were more promising for the reduction of the youth gang problem and were more successful than others. His work may have some insights for the future development of YOTs. Spergal (1995) stated that a detached worker is unable to deal with a complex structural problem, which requires the coordination of other strategies and relevant resources. It is necessary to work in a new social context with greater coordinating effort among diverse professionals and agencies.

As discussed above, most of the YOTs, ICYSCs and outreach teams for YNDs are concerned about the overlapping of services. To be frank, overlapping is better than having a service gap. Even the targets are overlapped, but the services can be different from other services. Each of the services has its own strengths and limitations. For example, ICYSCs have more resources than YOTs, and most of the ICYSCs have already gone through their modernisation process with their facilities more updated. These pools of resources would definitely be better than those of the YOTs. On the other hand, YOTs may have more information on community dynamics which workers of ICYSCs may not have the time to collect. To admit our own weaknesses and exercise our strengths are doors for cooperation.

To establish cooperation, a YOT can identify one or two high-risk areas and seek cooperation with the local ICYSCs or outreach team for YNDs. This cooperation should not be limited at the case level only, but should be in at a community level where more dimensions of intervention and possible methods of cooperation could be created.

Apart from the cooperation among agencies themselves, cooperation among different professionals is also required. Only street social work intervention may not be useful for contemporary street youth. Youth-at-risk are actually the young people who are vulnerable to external disadvantages and risks (Chui, 2001). This vulnerability goes beyond personal factors which need more than social work intervention.

In the past few years, some pilot projects have worked in this direction and have sought a combination of various programmes and professional specialisation, for example, "Extraordinary Body Check for Young Drug Abusers" (非常體驗) by the Hong Kong Playground Association. This project is a combination of social work intervention and medical intervention. This kind of cooperation should be continued, though the cooperation may not be easy because of the differences between different disciplines.

YOTs can successfully engage the unattached youth in the streets, but one of the difficulties is how to motivate the clients to commit to changes afterwards. One of the possible solutions is the exercise of social intervention not only in the streets, but also in other social contexts which are sometimes neglected but may be more effective than only work in the streets. These new social contexts may include schools where there maybe school-gangs conflicts, in a medical setting (e.g. clinic) when the youths seek medical service, or in the police station when the youth-at-risk is arrested. All these working contexts are places where we seldom try to exert intervention. In these contexts, the young people are usually in crisis or are experiencing feelings of stress, and are more easily motivated to change. Outreach workers are familiar with these contexts but sometimes overlook the utilisation of these contexts as means to conduct intervention. To make use of these contexts for intervention, a lot of coordinating may be involved, but if it is proven to be effective, we should have the courage and commitment to try. With the new contexts which arise, new strategies may develop.

Youth problems in Hong Kong may be different in various districts, but to a large extent, they have their own similarities, especially in the aspect of social disadvantages, such as the school system and the work environment. As suggested by Chui (2001), social workers should intervene concerning social disadvantages and the powerlessness caused by class, gender and age structure of society. In the past few years, outreach workers have tried to do some intervention concerning the social disadvantages of society. Ngai (2005) concluded that the outreach workers have already developed some strategies for tackling social disadvantages, such as seeking new allies for the development of community support networks, establishing a research centre for policy advocacy and coordinating with youth for social change. How to make these practices become a collective power and be one of our core working strategies should be one of our future goals.

We sometimes may encounter resistance or hesitation in allowing youth-at-risk to participate in our service development. Research conducted by Chui (2001) and Lee and Cham (2002) has shown that outreaching clients are ready to participate in the planning, implementing and evaluating of the service. The research has suggested that the outreach service should allow greater user-participation. If, on one hand, we advocate the rights of our clients, but on the other hand we ignore their rights of participation in the service, it would be a ridiculous practice. Allowing them to participate in the service can show our respect and trust in their abilities and also demonstrates their abilities and potentials to the community.

Conclusion

To appropriately design the OSW for youth-at-risk, we should base it on the contexts that we face. Without these considerations, the work may often get into a muddle. We also need to remember our core work focus, otherwise we will only be creating a programme rather than a service. It is believed that our future work should put more effort into coordinating among the local youth services and various disciplines. We need to work closely with local youth services to create synergy, to cooperate with various disciplines to cater for the multiple needs of youth, and to emancipate our youth from various oppressions. We need to remember the core mission of OSW—to reach out, to communicate, to understand and to connect street youth with our society.

References

Chui, W. H. (2001). "Users' Views of an Outreaching Social Work Team in Hong Kong," *International Social Work, Volume 44 (4)*, pp. 455–469.

Hong Kong Council of Social Service (1983). *Operation Manual for Outreaching Social Workers*. Hong Kong: HKCSS.

Lee, F. W. L. (1997). *Working With Natural Groups of Youth-at-Risk*. Hong Kong: Department of Social Work, Chinese University of Hong Kong.

Lee, F. W. L. (2002). *Development of Integrated Team Model for Children and Youth Services: To Be Or Not To Be?* Hong Kong: Department of Social Work and Social Administration, University of Hong Kong.

Lee, F. W. L. (2005). *Working With Youth-at-Risk in Hong Kong*. Hong Kong: Hong Kong University Press.

Lee, F. W. L. and Cham, L. M. Y. (2002). "The Possibility of Promoting User Participation in Working with High Risk Youth," *British Journal of Social Work, Volume 32*, pp. 71–92.

Ng, A. and Man, P. (1985). *The Report on the Evaluation of Outreaching Social Work*. Hong Kong: The Chinese University of Hong Kong.

Ngai, S. Y. (2005). "Breaking Through Barriers: The Political Actions of Hong Kong Outreach Youth Workers," *Hong Kong Journal of Social Work, Volume 39 (1/2)*, pp. 49–63.

Social Welfare Department (1998). *The Five Year Plan for Social Welfare Development in Hong Kong—Review 1998*. Hong Kong: Government Printer.

Spergel, I. A. (1995). *The Youth Gang Problem: A Community Approach*. New York: Oxford University Press.

Working Party on Review of Children and Youth Centre Services (1994). *Report on Review of Children and Youth Centre Service*. Hong Kong: Government Printer.

李文照（1996）。〈詮釋學觀照下的外展青少年工作〉。見何潔雲、李文照、莫泰基編，《青年工作新探索》。香港：中華書局。165–171頁。

李永年（2002）。〈綜合服務模式的青少年服務〉。見李永年編，《香港青少年問題廿一世紀初的現象、剖析與對策》。香港：香港大學出版社。121–133頁。

香港社會工作者總工會（2001）。《綜合服務隊街頭青少年群黨工作情況調查告》。香港：香港社會工作者總工會。（www.youthconcern.net）

（2002）。《反思再上路地區青少年外展社會工作隊同工分享》。香港：香港社會工作者總工會。（www.youthconcern.net）

（2002a）。《關注邊青服務專小組爭取「高危青少年區域專責隊」過程》。香港：香港社會工作者總工會。（www.youthconcern.net）

（2005）。《地區青少年外展社會工作隊同工分享會》。香港：香港社會工作者總工會。（www.youthconcern.net）

郭乃揚（1999）。〈縱觀外展二十年〉，《青年視野》。4期，15–27頁。

陳錦祥（1996）。〈青少年服務的改革與整合〉。見何潔雲、李文照、莫泰基編，《青年工作新探索》。香港：中華書局。123–132頁。

陳寶釗、郭乃揚、蔡錦發、曾永強（1997）。《香港外展社會工作縱橫》。香港：集賢社。

陳寶釗（2003）。〈外展社工服務的機遇〉，《香港中華基督教青年會專題導報》。39期，10–17頁。

盧鐵榮（1990）。〈從歷史看外展工作的未來〉。見香港社會服務聯會兒童及青少年部編，《過渡期的青少年服務：服務資料彙編》。香港：香港社會服務聯會。46–58頁。

《明報》（2005）。〈近四成濫藥青年未老先衰，團體促增驗身服務警醒青年毒品禍害〉。專訊，4月18日。

OVERNIGHT OUTREACHING SERVICE FOR YOUNG NIGHT DRIFTERS

Chi-man CHOW

2

Introduction

Starting from September 2001, 18 Overnight Outreaching Service Teams for Young Night Drifters (YNDs Teams) have been conducting the YND Service over the territory. Close to 50 social workers of the 18 teams have travelled around their service areas to identify and provide services for the young night drifters (YNDs). The YNDs Service is said to serve a very important function of making connection with groups of youth-at-risk who have otherwise been overlooked by the conventional daytime service. It is also to link up with mainstream young people and other support services. But unfortunately, it is noted that the development of the YND Service has been overlooked in our social welfare context in the previous six-year provision of service.

A number of misconceptions about its service nature and operation, and even its funding source, are found especially at the initial service establishment. There had been a misconception that the YND Service would only be operated for two to three years as a pilot project and would not become a regular provision. In fact, the YND Service is a regular service under the subvention of Social Welfare Department (SWD) of the Government. Questions have been raised by the public and even some social work practitioners such as, what is the service operation and provision of the YND Service? How effective is it in performing its significant role in integrating with mainstream services? What are the service needs of the YNDs? What is the future development of the YND Service?

In order to allow concerned persons to have a more comprehensive view of the YND Service, experience from the establishment of the service, the exploration of service provision, its changes, and its development will be discussed in this chapter. How the YND Service has developed, what kinds of difficulties have been encountered and overcome, what strategies have been used to tackle the hardships, and the suggested direction for its future development will be discussed in the following sections.

A Brief History of the YND Service

Service for the YNDs was initially introduced into Hong Kong by Youth Outreach in the early 1990s as a self-financed service. At that time, there was much concern about the runaway and homeless teenagers who hung around public places overnight and created much public nuisance and behaved in an unruly manner. The Youth Outreach formed an outreach team to travel around the territory to identify those runaway and homeless young people under the age of 18. The workers of the Team initiated contact with them and brought the YNDs back to their hostel if necessary. This action was based on the rationale that there was potential danger for a youngster in hanging around overnight and engaging in nighttime drifting activities.

In May 1996, the Chinese University of Hong Kong (CUHK) was commissioned to conduct a study titled "An Exploration of the Risk and Protective Factors of Juvenile Gangs and Runaway Youth in Hong Kong" (Tang and Davis, 1996) by the Inter-departmental Working Group on Services for Youth at Risk of the (then) Health Bureau and the Standing Committee of Young Offenders of the Central Fight Crime Committee of the Government. With reference to one of the recommendations from the research, a two-year experimental pilot project named "Youth Mobile Teams" (YMTs) was then established to serve the YNDs of Kowloon, Hong Kong Island and the New Territories in October 1997 (Lee, 1999). Two Non-governmental Organisations (NGOs), the Youth Outreach (YO) and the Hong Kong Federation of Youth Groups (HKFYG), were funded by the Social Welfare Department (SWD) and ran the experimental pilot project respectively on Hong Kong Island and Kowloon and the New Territories so as to provide on-the-spot crisis and short-term intervention to the YNDs (Youth Mobile Team, 1999). Besides evaluating the effectiveness and possibilities of this new service mode, this project also aimed to assess the needs of the YNDs. Lee and Tang (1999) of CUHK were commissioned to do the evaluation study.

The evaluation study indicated that there were around 10,000 to 20,000 YNDs hanging around in open premises every night and that 35–55% of them had service needs (Lee and Tang, 1999). After considering the recommendations from the assessment report, the SWD decided to establish YND Service in the territory. Eighteen Overnight Outreaching Service Teams for Young Night Drifters (YND Teams) have been set up by different NGOs over the territory under the subvention of the SWD with the aim of meeting the service demand of the YNDs since September 2001.

Regarding the policy of providing one-stop centre-based, school social work and outreach service for young people by a team of social workers in a holistic and integrated manner, the 18 YND Teams, with three manpower resources and a lump sum of operational expenses, are operated among and attached to 18 Integrated Children and Youth Services Centres (ICYSCs) according to the locality base throughout the territory.

After providing the services for YNDs for four years since 2001, the SWD has allocated additional manpower resources by providing 2/3 additional workers for each YND Team in accordance with the assessed number of juvenile delinquents of the 18 communities served in August 2005 (Overnight Youth Outreaching Service, 2003).

Service Contents of YND Teams

The operation hours of different YND Teams will have slight differences, but generally, they are from 10:00p.m. to 6:00a.m. of the following day. Each Team is equipped with a private car to facilitate its touring around the service community for identifying YNDs. During the service hours, the Team will drive around the community, especially the hot spots for YNDs, and carry out its services, such as group or individual counselling, escorting to homes, service introduction, etc. Some cases may need follow-ups and be referred to daytime services, e.g. family service, school social work service and centre service, etc. (PROJECT SINEWS, 2004).

Various Team Formation

The establishment of the YND Teams was put forth under the implementation of the Lump Sum Grant. Responsible NGOs have provided a standard manning ratio (three manpower) and operational expenses to manage their YND Teams. The NGOs can have their own autonomy in arranging their manpower with reference to their service, provided they can accomplish the operational objectives and standards of the Funding and Service Agreement (FSA) with the Government (Social Welfare Department, 2001 and 2003). Through the implementation of FSA, the SWD can monitor the services with respect to criteria such as the categorisation of service targets, the operational hours of the service, the service effectiveness, etc. Apart from that, the NGOs can develop their service uniqueness regarding the working approach, service characteristics, and concerns in accordance with the features of the communities served. As a result, there are variations on the actual manpower deployment and the mode of operation, such as working strategies employed among the 18 YND Teams. There have been some discussions and cooperation concerning the service provision, modes of service operation and difficulties in service delivery, and the interpretation of FSA Standards in the supervisory meetings of YND Teams. The responses of the SWD emphasise the allowing of diversification of service provision among NGOs under the Lump Sum Grant arrangement.

To a certain extent, YND Teams have been given autonomy to develop their service in a flexible manner, but some doubts exist concerning the service implementation in actual practice. Is the service development beneficial with the autonomy allowed by the SWD? Are there any variations between the views of the SWD and the frontline workers (the former is focused on enhancing the effectiveness of service management, while the latter emphasises a comprehensive and holistic development of the YND Service)? Nevertheless, the SWD has considered individual priorities and concerns of different YND Teams and incorporated them into the standard performance to be accomplished in their FSA respectively. Thus, there are differences in the standards of the FSA of the 18 YND Teams. Some concentrate on the scope of Output Standards, while others concentrate on the scope of Outcome Standards.

Constraint of Operating Hours

The operating hours of YND Teams in providing direct service have been strictly set by the SWD as one of the output standards. Basically, a total number of 2,505 hours of direct contact yearly has to be met as the minimum standard for each YND Team. In order to achieve this standard, each worker of a YND Team has to provide at least three overnight outreach services under an 8-hour service operation (nearly half of his weekly working hours) so as to meet this output standard. So, it was quite common that each YND Team has provided its service for at least three overnights which are mainly from Thursday to Sunday (10:00p.m. to 6:00a.m.) every week.

After accumulating some practice experience, most YND Teams have commonly found that the number of YNDs decreases after 3:00a.m. After increasing the manpower of the YND Service in 2005, every YND Team now has five or six workers. The output standard of direct contact hours is thus proportionally increased to either 4,175 or 5,010 yearly. All YND Teams have expanded their operations, ranging from five to seven overnight outreach services, and have shortened the operation time till 3:00a.m. or 4:00a.m. to provide more effective service.

In respect to the output standard, it defines the direct contact hours and reflects the direct service for the YNDs during the overnight period, but it neglects other related parts of the work of the YND Teams, especially their contribution in helping or referring YNDs in the daytime. In addition, it dominates the proportion of time allocation of the YND workers and limits other scopes of the service development. It is difficult both to have the service development and to meet the output standard under such constraint. It is hope that there will be room for improvement.

Ambiguity in Functions

With regard to the abovementioned output and outcome standards, the SWD is concerned about the service flow of the referral or transferral of cases of YNDs and the successful connection of YNDs in receiving the mainstream services. Other than handling on-the-spot crisis, the main function of YND Teams is to channel the YNDs back into the mainstream youth services as expected. Besides providing direct service for the YNDs, all YND Teams have to spend a great deal of time in connecting with appropriate mainstream youth services in the district, namely, the ICYSCs, the District Youth Outreaching Teams, the School Social Work Service, etc. Apart from case referral of the YNDs, a variety of formal contacts have been adopted to build up cooperative working relationships and referral networks through service introduction, inter-district service-sharing meetings, meetings for sharing the youth phenomena in the district, and organising joint functions and activities for the YNDs. Among the output standards, it is found that the counting of time spent on these activities is the major headache for most YND Teams. There are three main factors giving rise to such difficulties.

Firstly, there are different perceptions concerning the definition of transferrals or referrals. Numerous questions have been raised by frontline workers regarding these, and it has been repeatedly discussed in the supervisory meetings. Some major questions include how to define a successful referral or transferal, and to what extent should YND workers have to be involved in successful transferrals or referrals. Although an effort to clarify this output standard has been made with the authority concerned, i.e. the SWD, there is still a lack of clear guidelines. With respect to the current circumstances, all 18 YND Teams make up their own guidelines to report the statistics according to the standard, so as to incorporate different areas of concern and degree of intervention in service delivery, and to reflect the actual work done.

Secondly, it is definitely advantageous for the workers to have a thorough exploration and assessment of needs of the YNDs before making transferrals and referrals. Most of the crises, e.g. running away from home, suspected child abuse, and molestation or assault, often are accompanied by clear and specific needs which make the referral or transferal processes easier. However, crises happen incidentally, but not frequently. Most of time, the YND workers have to expend a great deal of time to establish a trusting working relationship with the YNDs who conceal their needs from workers, have no obvious motivation in receiving assistance and show reluctance in respect to contact with a social worker. Once a trusting working relationship between the YNDs and the workers has been built up, they may have expectations with respect to the workers. It would be difficult for them to accept assistance from workers of other mainstream services, and this situation causes more difficulties in making transferrals or referrals.

Last but not least, as we all know, there is a discrepancy between the lifestyle pattern of the YNDs and the operation hours of the other mainstream services, which adds a great many difficulties in making appropriate transferrals and referrals of the YNDs. In practice, even when the YNDs have been matched with and transferred or referred to the appropriate mainstream services successfully, hardships concerning follow-up contact of the YNDs during the daytime by the mainstream services are encountered. Due to such discontinuous contacts, some of the YND cases have to be terminated by the concerned mainstream services. It would be beneficial if some individual mainstream services which operate during the daytime considered this constraint and were willing to adjust their operating hours so as to meet the daily schedule and ever-changing needs of the YNDs. Some of them even collaborate with YND Teams to provide special service and launch activities late at night with the aim of establishing an initial working relationship with the YNDs.

Transformation in Service Delivery

Seen from the perspective of crisis prevention, it is reasonable for the FSA of YND Service to state that the service target of YND Teams should be "young people under the age of 18 who loiter or drift in the street at late hours at night." In retrospect, at the time of the experimental pilot project of the YND service in 1997, the two YMTs had to serve the YNDs throughout the entire territory. It would be more effective for them to focus on certain districts where the phenomenon of YNDs prevails. However, the service boundary has become limited after the establishing of the 18 YND Teams in the territory. There is an insufficient number of service targets who are under the age of 18 in certain districts as the service target is scaled down. The YND Teams have then to concentrate on the activities of other YND groups who are over 18 years of age as well.

Comparing the past and present behaviour and phenomena of the YNDs, there were no obvious changes. As crisis-handling is an incidental intervention in the service delivery, the focus of YND Service has been gradually shifted to work with more constant groups of YNDs. Moreover, working with youth who engage in night-drifting behaviour also arouses the concern of the YND Teams. It is apparent that the YND Service has been transformed from a mode of crisis intervention for YNDs to a more predominantly developmental and preventive model. Different YND Teams have employed various approaches and introduced different means to launch programmes and activities to meet the specific needs and characteristics of the YND groups they serve. For instance, some YND Teams have made use of the extension of operating hours of some stadiums of the Leisure and Cultural Services Department to organise programmes such as dancing, X-games activities, indoor training, and exhibitions.

Judging by the transformation of the service delivery mode, it cannot be denied that the practitioners of YNDs have performed a flexible role and provided a more responsive service toward the needs of the YNDs in an appropriate manner. In spite of this, there is still discrepancy between the original service planning and the actual practice. For example, the SWD had allocated additional resources to the Hong Kong Student Aids Society to increase the number of placements in the hostel, with the aim of acting as a supportive service for the YNDs at the initial operational phase of the YND Service. But it was found that the utilisation rate for the placements in the hostel was low compared with the original anticipation in the service planning. With reference to the actual service operation and delivery and the proven service-usage discrepancy, does it imply that the existing FSA standard may not be a good indicator?

In addition, the roles of the YND Service have become more than a channel to connect the YNDs into other mainstream services, as the YND Service has expanded to a more comprehensive service and has adopted different intervention approaches and modes of service-delivery including the providing of casework service and launching of special programmes. Such transformation has had a direct influence on the time allocation of YND workers as they have both to meet an increasing demand for daytime work and to perform the required overnight outreach duty. Perhaps, it is an appropriate time for the SWD to conduct a thorough review on whether the output standard of YND Service may not reflect the real practice.

Instability in Manpower

The establishment of the 18 YND Teams was done at a time when the reduction of expenses and resources in the social welfare context was prevalent. There was a great reduction of posts and salaries of social workers, and social work posts were limited. Though some individual NGOs had deployed some experienced social workers to conduct YND service, owing to the unappealing nature of working overnight, not many experienced workers had a keen interest in it. Thus, the post of an YND worker could mainly be regarded as a stepping stone by social work graduates.

With limited working experience, e.g. on crisis intervention, lack of skills in relationship building and support and guidance, the new and inexperienced workers could only perform their basic duty as overnight outreach workers, without contribution to their professional development. When opportunities arose, they withdrew and resigned from their work with YNDs, and changed to working in daytime mainstream services because of the unfavourable conditions of working overnight for an unattractive salary. As a result, the turnover of YND workers was very frequent—lots of new faces came and went. The frequent turnover of YND workers has negative impact on the service operation, the accumulation of work experience, and the service development.

The YND Service has found increasing difficulty in recruiting workers as more posts (and opportunities) have been provided in other mainstream services in recent years. Taking the additional manpower resource allocation in August 2005 as an example, it has been revealed that a total of 12 YND Teams were short of workers according to the manpower standard in the financial year 2006–07. Some YND Teams had only half of the manpower to provide the service over a long period of time. With reference to the Lump Sum Grant arrangement, the agreed service output standards between the SWD and the Teams could not be deducted in proportion to unfilled vacancies. The concerned NGOs/YND Teams have had to shoulder the responsibility in dealing with the shortage of manpower and other unstable factors of service operation under such practice. The shortage of YND workers results in an adverse effect on the routine service operation, and also results in a failure to meet the FSA Standards, especially concerning the output standard of the total number of direct contact hours.

In fact, the respective NGOs/YND Teams have made their best effort in trying to tackle the problem of the unstable manpower. Some of them have employed more staff to prepare for the frequent resignation of workers, while others have offered an increase in salary or travelling allowance so as to make the overnight work more attractive. But no obvious effect was created through such measures. Moreover, the YND Teams have tried to change their strategies from the perspective of service integration in the hope of maintaining a stable manpower for service provision.

In theory, the YND Service is an integral part of an ICYSC, and the respective ICYSC has to perform the key functions of planning the overall YND Service implementation with thorough and holistic consideration of its service operation, distribution of manpower, and use of resources. However, this is not the case in practice. All 18 YND Teams have adopted either a semi-independent or a fully independent mode of service operation at the start-up. Designated YND workers of the Teams are responsible for the overall management of the YND service that is independent from the service operation and division of work of the ICYSCs to which the Teams are attached. In the early years of the service, some workers from the ICYSCs assisted in providing direct overnight outreach service from time to time in order to share the burden of the YND Teams. But such a mode was certainly not a form of service integration. It can only be concluded that this was some sort of support and assistance from the concerned ICYSCs.

But it is considered that service integration is a way for YND Teams to minimise the adverse impacts of unstable manpower. At present, there are variations in the mode of service integration which are different from the originally planned service integration of the ICYSCs. Some YND Teams have merged with the District Youth Outreaching Teams (YOTs) as they share a lot of commonalities, such as having the same service boundaries, and having similar nature of service and characteristics of service target; and it would be easier for them to re-distribute the work after the merging and integration of the two services. Some YND Teams merge with the outreach workers of the ICYSCs to which they are attached, as the two services have a similar nature of work and adopt similar approaches to the service target.

Of course, there are merits to service integration. Firstly, the merging of services, either with the YOTs or the ICYSCs, can guarantee a larger and stable manpower pool for the YND Teams that will minimise the negative impacts of lack of manpower, meet the output standard of the FSA, and reduce pressure on the workers. Secondly, such service merging can benefit the newcomers in the field. As their working hours of overnight work are now shared by more workers, they have more opportunities to generate and consolidate their work experience for professional development. With greater job satisfaction and more assurance of the value of their work, their desire to change jobs is lowered, which in turn can help to stabilise the manpower situation.

The above-described merging of services should be viewed as a means to solve the loss of manpower from the administration. The idea of the merging of services for YND Service is based on consideration of the service development of the YND service. During meetings of supervisors and YND teams, lots of comments have been made on the positive influence and effectiveness of the YND Service after merging. But we seem to focus too much on the YND Service. The impact on YOTs and ICYSCs after merging is being neglected. Concerned parties should take further heed of evaluating the possible impact on YOTs and ICYSCs. Is the service-merging a win-win strategy for the service development of YOTs, ICYSCs, as well as the YND Service? To what extent are the original work duties affected for workers of YOTs and ICYSCs after the merging? It is important to consider how to balance the stability of the manpower of YOTs and ICYSCs, as well as the YND Service, as it has been found that some workers of YOTs and ICYSCs have considered changing their present job after the merging (Wong, 2007).

Conclusion: Future Development of the YND Service

Hong Kong is a modern city with lots of overnight convenience stores, fast-food shops, and entertainment establishments. With the well-established traffic network in the territory that provides overnight service, it is convenient for people to access places wherever they want at any time, even after midnight. It is common for people to involve themselves in nocturnal activities indoors and outdoors. This living pattern and culture has gradually met the unique needs of people living such a lifestyle (Chan, 2002).

In the past, the main intervention objective of the YND service was focused on bringing the YNDs back to the "normal" living pattern of daytime. However, YND workers no longer take negative view of the nocturnal pattern of the YNDs. It is believed that this nocturnal pattern is inevitable and it would be better to help the YNDs to tackle the problems they encounter in their daily lives. Apart from focusing its core concern on the potential risks of the YNDs who engage in the nocturnal activities and the related negative influences caused, the YND Service should also extend its services to other youth groups like the working youth who also engage in nocturnal activities. If the changing lifestyle pattern of Hong Kong people is recognised, the service development of the YND Service will have greater scope in the future. More studies can be conducted to increase our understanding of the nightlife pattern of Hong Kong young people as well as how to improve the provision of the YND Service effectively. If the SWD can allow the concerned NGOs/YND Teams to have more scope for innovative service delivery, e.g. adopting other means for monitoring service effectiveness, reducing some output standards that hinder service delivery, conducting a comprehensive review on the YND Service, and considering the possibility of introducing new services to meet the ever-increasing needs of the nighttime service, it will definitely bring many benefits for YNDs, and a new scope of development of the YND Service can be possible.

In this chapter, we have briefly discussed the process of service development and the transformation of the YND service operation. Undoubtedly, tremendous efforts have been made by YND practitioners and the concerned NGOs/YND Teams to overcome the problems and difficulties encountered in service delivery. In respect to the problems of service operation and the frequent turnover of staff that has resulted in an unstable manpower, meeting the output standard of the FSA has become the top concern. Further development of the service, exploration of the appropriate mode of service delivery, and assessment on service effectiveness have been underemphasised. With the service transformation, the role and functions of the YND Service have become rather unclear. Moreover, the function of the YND Service in meeting the developmental and preventive needs of young people and YNDs has been overridden by the emphasis on crisis intervention and the remedial function of the service. It is time for the YND Service to assess its roles and functions for the YNDs.

References

Lee, F. W. L. (1999). "Service for Young Night Drifters in Hong Kong—The Youth Mobile Teams: An Inclusion Movement?" *Promoting Inclusion—Redressing Exclusion: The Social Work Challenge.* (Joint Conference AASW, IFSW, APASWE, AASWWE) (Conference Proceedings Volume 2) (pp. 35–40).

Lee, F. W. L. and Tang, C. S. K. (1999). *Evaluation Study of Youth Mobile Team Service for Young Night Drifters.* Hong Kong: Authors.

Social Welfare Department (2001). *The Funding and Service Agreement (Lump Sum Grant) for Integrated Teams of Young People Services with Service for Young Night Drifters.* Hong Kong: Social Welfare Department.

Social Welfare Department (2003). *The Funding and Service Agreement (Lump Sum Grant) for Integrated Teams of Young People Services with Service for Young Night Drifters.* Hong Kong: Social Welfare Department.

Tang, C. S. K. and Davis, C. (1996). *An Exploration of the Risk and Protective Factors of Juvenile Gangs and Runaway Youth in Hong Kong*. Hong Kong: Authors.

Wong, C. S. Y. (2007). *Study on Job Satisfaction and Staff Turnover of District Youth Outreaching Social Work Teams (YOTs) in Hong Kong*. (Unpublished M.Soc.Sc. Dissertation) Hong Kong: University of Hong Kong.

深宵青少年外展服務（2003）。《EXPO資料冊》。全港深宵外展服務督導主任會議。

青少年流動工作隊（星夜計劃）（1999）。《星夜計劃報告書，97–99》。香港:香港青年協會。

星鳥計劃（Project Sinews）（2004）。《從星夜走到黎明》。香港:香港青少年服務處。

陳達湘（2002）。《香港夜青與其家庭、學校和朋輩體系的關係，與及其深宵活動模式的變化研究摘要》。香港：協青社。

3

COMMUNITY SUPPORT SERVICE SCHEME

Gary Kin-lam YUNG and Koon-mei LEE

In October 1994, the Social Welfare Department (SWD) started to subvent the Community Support Service Scheme (CSSS) (Fight Crime Committee, 1996; Lo, 1998; Lo *et al.*, 2001). CSSS originated from the Project Phoenix (PP)—Counselling Service. PP was a 1992 one-man-band pioneer non-subvented counselling project for juvenile offenders initiated by Methodist Centre in cooperation with the Wan Chai Police Station. The Wan Chai Police Station referred youngsters who were cautioned under the Police Superintendent's Discretion Scheme (PSDS) to Methodist Centre for counselling and follow-up services (Lo and Kam, 1994). The idea behind PP had caught attention and recognition from the community and the Government. Thus, in 1994, the SWD expanded its service scope and began to subvent Project Phoenix—CSSS of Methodist Centre to serve cautioned youth in Hong Kong Island and outlying islands. By then, the manpower of PP or CSSSs had increased from one social worker to five professional social workers.

The SWD itself also runs two units of CSSS at Kowloon East and Kowloon West for young probationers, and it has subvented the Hong Kong Federation of Youth Groups to run another unit of CSSS at the New Territories West region since 1994. All the service users of different units of CSSS were the review research targets of Lo *et al.* (1997). The evaluation research of Lo *et al.* (1997) confirmed the effectiveness of CSSSs. All Schemes became long-term subvented services in 1998. The research also recommended setting up more CSSSs to help youth-at-risk (YAR), so that cautioned juveniles under PSDS in the whole territory of Hong Kong could be served. In early 2001, the SWD announced that "Care for the Youth-at-Risk" would be the main theme of forthcoming youth services. In October 2001, three more units of CSSS, each with four professional social workers, by Non-governmental Organisations (NGOs), covering Kowloon East, Kowloon West and New Territories East regions, were set up. The three new CSSSs were attached with respective agencies' Integrated Children and Youth Services Centres (ICYSCs). For better service synergy, subsequently, the five CSSS units of NGOs are all attached to their mother agencies' existing ICYSCs.

The Chief Executive's Policy Address in 2005 highlighted helping the poor and the needy. YAR of CSSSs was one of the targets being identified as needy. Double manpower resources were pooled into CSSSs in August of 2005. Now each unit of the NGOs' CSSS has eight to ten professional social workers serving its respective region.

This chapter aims to introduce the CSSS of NGOs in Hong Kong, including its rationale, purposes, theoretical framework, practices and service impacts. Difficulties being encountered and a look ahead will be discussed in the latter half. As PP is the prototype, examples and experience from it will be quoted throughout the chapter as references.

Rationale for the Initiative (PP): Filling up the Service Gap

The emergence of different initiatives of youth services in Hong Kong has always been associated with the occurrence of juvenile delinquency (Cheung, 1993; Lee, 2005; Lee, 2001; Ng, 1980 and 1994; Ng *et al.*, 1975; Vagg *et al.*, 1995). The publication of a Green Paper on "Personal Social Work among Young People" in 1977 concretised the provision of school social work service, outreaching service and family life education service for delinquency prevention. It is believed that intervention for strengthening the social systems of school, peers, family and other social organisations is necessary to improve young people's capacity in adapting to society.

In the early 1990s, the upsurge of juvenile crime had threatened the public. The outcry for stronger supportive services to YAR was made. This led to the speedy expansion of some pilot schemes, such as PP, night-time outreaching service for young night drifters (Lee, 1996).

In 1992, Methodist Centre pioneered inviting police officers of Wan Chai Police Station to refer law-breaking cautioned youth for social work follow-up services. It was a benchmark breakthrough of a multi-disciplinary approach for serving the welfare of YAR. According to subvented youth service classification, a cautioned youth service could not fall into any formal category of youth service at that time. Outreaching services may occasionally come across a portion of cautioned youth, but no direct social service can be tapped for that service target. The rationale for launching PP was to fill up the identified service gap, and thus, YAR cautioned under PSDS could be served. A direct referral system from Police was then set up. PP offered professional intervention for the cautioned youth and they were empowered to build up relationship with their families and schools, as well as peers. They were also encouraged to explore and develop their potential to their utmost and dedicate themselves to the community. Given the fact that resources are always short in supply, setting up service priorities and targeting the services for those with greatest needs and risks have always been aims of the service. The Project Phoenix—Counselling Service has been renamed as Project Phoenix—Community Support Service Scheme after receiving SWD subvention since 1994. Compared to the 1970s' "Personal Social Work among Young People," the Hong Kong Government seemed to have entered into a new phase of rationale concerning "Community Support Mode for Young People" in the 1990s. A multi-disciplinary working approach and cooperation have been strongly stressed in social services.

Purposes and Objectives of CSSS: Reduced Recidivism and Life Enrichment

The purposes and objectives of all NGOs' units of CSSS are more or less the same as outlined in the Funding Service Agreement (FSA) of SWD in 2005.

The ultimate purposes of CSSS are:

1. To assist targeted young people to re-integrate into the community;
2. To eliminate their deviant and unlawful behaviour; and
3. To reduce their likelihood of law infringement.

The objectives of working with these young people are:

1. To reintegrate the targeted children and youth into the education system or to initiate their entrance into work force;
2. To help them to develop socially acceptable behaviour;
3. To redirect their energies into constructive and legitimate channels;
4. To lead them to become law-abiding persons; and
5. To enhance their development through strengthening the community support network.

Moreover, besides a series of output indicators, the SWD has added two outcome indicators on the FSA, i.e. more than 90% of the service targets have no recidivism during the supervision period and more than 85% of the service targets remain in either study or work at the time of closing the cases. The FSA symbolises the funding body (SWD) and society have requests and requirements on the effectiveness and accountability of the service.

The three purposes stated in the FSA clearly show that the function of CSSS is to reduce cautioned youth's recidivism. Though all referred cautioned youth present similar problems—law-breaking behaviour—each of them is unique with different needs. Their law-breaking behaviour may be caused by different reasons. In practice, we have to be both task-oriented, helping the youth to be law-abiding and also to be person-oriented, and enhancing their life development through strengthening their community support systems. To have "heart" and commitment in helping our targeted youth is of the utmost importance in carrying out successful CSSS.

Theoretical Framework: Longitudinal (Crisis Intervention Theory) Vs. Horizontal (Social Bond/ACIB Theory)

Helping YAR immediately after their cautioning is most powerful and significant. We must value that valuable intervention moment, and Crisis Intervention Theory (CIT) is most applicable. We refer to it as "longitudinal theoretical account" in respect to CSSS. Moreover, closely appreciating the time-frame, CIT is complemented by horizontal Social Bond Theory (A-Attachment, C-Commitment, I-Involvement, B-Belief) (Hirschi, 1969). The ACIB Theory gives details of the intervention map while the YAR are assisted to go beyond the difficult crisis time.

Longitudinal Account: Crisis Intervention Theory

All of the referred YAR have been arrested by the police and have experienced PSDS (a precipitating event), and thus, most of their responses are similar to persons facing crises, i.e. helplessness, anxiety, anger and confusion. Crisis is a period of disequilibrium and decreased functioning as a result of an event or situation that creates a significant problem which cannot be resolved by using familiar coping strategies. The crisis is not the event itself, but rather the individuals' perceptions of and responses to the situation. Three core components of CIT include a precipitating event, client perception of the event, and the client's usual coping methods (Aguilera and Messick, 1987; Golan, 1978; Parad, 1971; Parry, 1990; Roberts, 2000). CSSSs provide direct and timely assistance and intervention (e.g. comfort, liaison with family, clarification of procedure involved, etc.). After receiving these assistances, the targeted youth find it easier to resume functioning and have greater motivation to change. The following figure (Figure 3.1) explains the transformation path of the YAR with unlawful behaviour.

Most of the cautioned youth said that they had not considered the seriousness of their behaviour prior to the arrests. They usually

Figure 3.1: Crisis Intervention Path on Youth-at-risk with Unlawful Behaviour

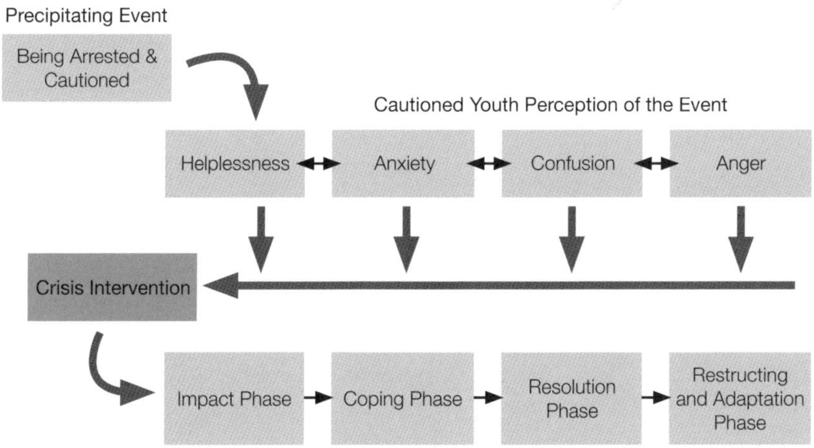

are worried, confused and helpless when they are experiencing PSDS, while their parents are shocked, disappointed and blame themselves. At this stage (Impact Phase), we have to understand individual youths and their parents' perceptions of and reactions to the events of the arrest. Then, we can move to the Coping Phase. Resources are mobilised with guided complemented ACIB intervention direction to set up contract and working goals (Resolution Phase) with the YAR when they want to strengthen themselves and become law-abiding for the sake of their future. Putting working goals into action and practice is the most crucial step that YAR can experience in the success of their behavioural change. Helping the YAR to restructure their positive-change experience (Reconstructing and Adaptation Phase) can reinforce some to adapt and overcome the crises of the arrests and to face future similar challenges and risks. The above crisis intervention transformation path is ideal in conceptualisation. In reality, some YAR may hesitate or be unwilling to change. We have to be patient and flexible enough to understand the underlying reasons that obstruct them from changing. Most of the YAR prefer to move beyond the offending events, but have inadequate confidence. This situation requires the expertise and skills of a concerned social worker in the helping process. The four phases of intervention go back and forth, while making use of critical moments in a timely manner and wisely plays an important role in the process.

Horizontal Account: ACIB Theory

Five units of NGO's CSSS have similar missions and beliefs in working with YAR. To summarise, CSSSs provide counselling services, family and peers support services, and voluntary and community support services for unlawful youth. According to the leaflet of each CSSS (BGCA, 2006; ELCHK, 2006; HKPA, 2006; HKYFG, 2004; MC, 2006), none of the unit, except MC (PP), has summarised and spelt out the theoretical framework behind the service. Thus, the following will introduce the PP horizontal conceptual framework of ACIB, which may not account for the theoretical frameworks employed by all NGOs' CSSS units, but we can use it as a reference for what the CSSS conceptual framework will likely be.

Numerous scholars have explored the causes of juvenile delinquency (Cheung, 1993; Cheung and Ng, 1988; Jang and Smith, 1997; Krohn *et al.*, 1996; Lam, 1998; Lee, 1996 and 2005; Lee, 2001; Ng *et al.*, 1975; Weis *et al.*, 1996; Wong, 1997 and 1999; Wong *et al.*, 1995), however, no single theory is comprehensive enough to explain the phenomenon. Meanwhile, the explanatory power increases when more of the major theories are integrated (Elliott *et al.*, 1985; Thornberry, 1987; Wong, 1999).

ACIB Theory originated from the Social Bond Theory of Hirschi (1969), while some modifications have been made to strengthen the explanation. In the Theory, four elements—Attachment, Commitment, Involvement and Belief—are emphasised as essential in creating the bond. PP focuses on enhancing the YAR attachment to conventional others; commitment to social values and norms;

Figure 3.2: Application of ACIB Theory on Youth-at-risk with Unlawful Behaviour

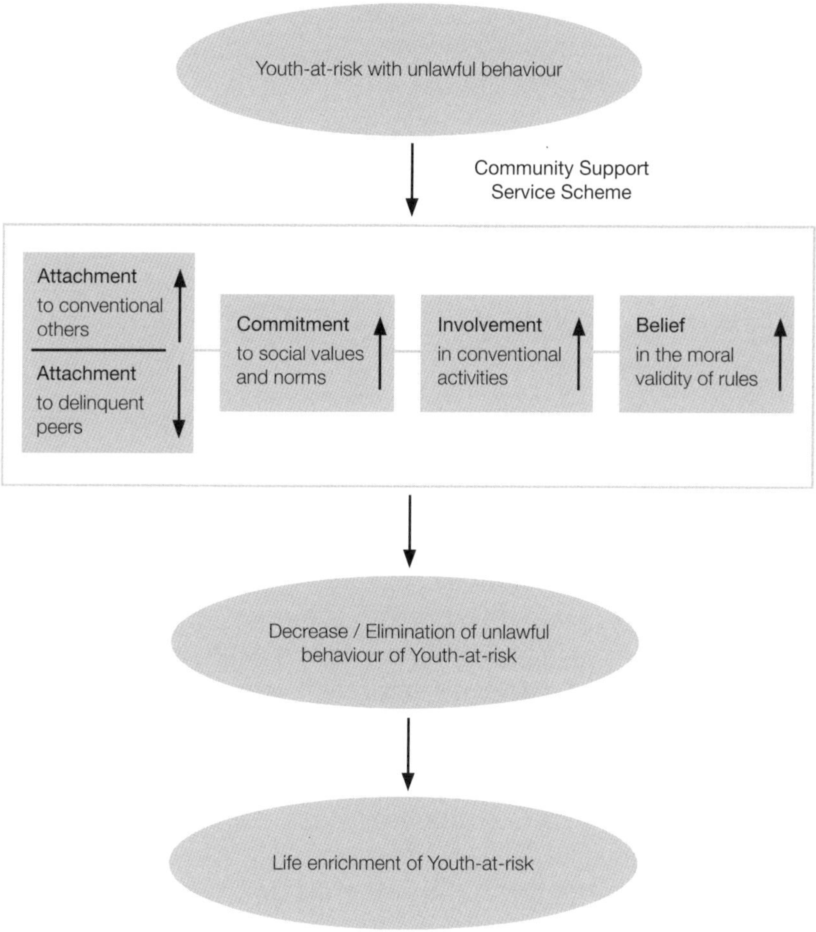

involvement in conventional activities and belief in the moral validity of rules, while discouraging their attachment to delinquent peers. An integrated model suggests that weakened bonds set the stage for delinquent behaviour, and such behaviour needs to be learned and reinforced before it is enacted. Attachment to delinquent peers is directly related to delinquency (Thornberry *et al.*, 1991; Trojanowicz and Morash, 1992). Before any intervention, strengths of the

Figure 3.3: Starfish Wisdom

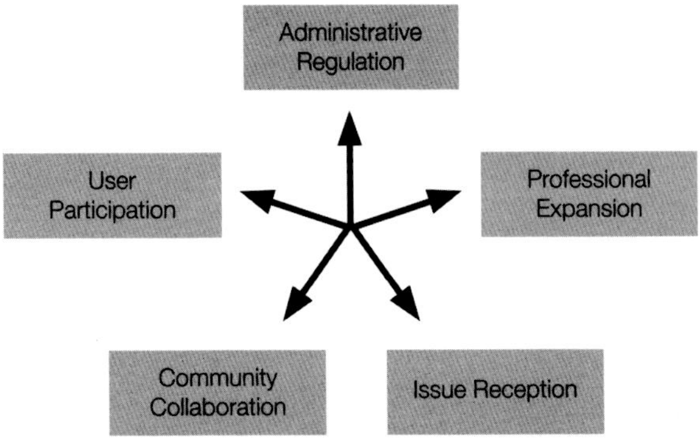

targeted youth are empowered. Each element co-exists and together they serve as a mind map for intervention. As every youngster is unique, we have to be flexible and sensible, together with youngsters' readiness for change; by then the intervention of the Scheme would be more effective.

By joining the CSSS, the unlawful behaviour of the YAR would be decreased or eliminated and their lives would also be enriched. The ACIB Theory guiding the horizontal intervention of CSSS is presented in Figure 3.2.

Operation and Practice: Starfish Wisdom

In practice, five aspects are further explained and discussed. The five aspects are: administrative regulation, user participation, professional expansion, community collaboration, and issue reception. They are referred to as "Starfish (five angles) Wisdom," meaning that it cannot be counted as "wisdom" if any one of the "five angles" is missing. Figure 3.3 depicts the five aspects of "Starfish Wisdom."

Administrative Regulation refers to the basic and necessary design layout of the service. Different units of CSSS have their own service layout. At PP, the service layout refers to Diversified Case Management Model (DCMM) (Lo, 1998; Lo and Lee, 2006; Lo *et al.*, 2001). DCMM has evolved as time has gone by and enriched as practical wisdom has been accumulated. The most up-to-date version of DCMM is presented in Figure 3.4.

With close collaboration with police officers, when the Police Superintendents have been scheduled to exercise cautions, the police detectives will phone the CSSS unit in advance, and thus intake appointments can then be scheduled. For PP, every Tuesday afternoon is reserved for intake. For basic assessment of the urgency and nature of the referred youth, each unit of CSSS has their own "Intake Assessment Tool." Usually four dimensions—family, schooling or career, peers, and behaviour—will be explored and necessary actions will then be taken afterwards. For example, if the YAR has been under PSDS prior to the recent cautioning, immediate follow-up will be given. On the other hand, if the YAR has already received the services of another agency, the responsible case worker will liaise with those in the supporting profession to discuss the welfare and working plan for the YAR. If service is assessed as having been duplicated, the CSSS unit may not open the intake case as a long-term case. Resources can be more concentrated and effectively used for the cautioned youth-in-need. A sample of the brief intake assessment form is described in Figure 3.5.

CSSS employs casework as its central work, though some high-risk cases require more intensive and in-depth intervention, while some low-risk cases may require a shorter period of follow-up. Each referred YAR is assigned to a responsible social worker by the supervisor, and casework services are provided. During the intervention process of casework, groups and community networking activities are also organised for the YAR (cases) who need them. An integrated community-based working approach has been adopted. Moreover, an orientation day is an added new practice since 2004. All newly referred YAR and their parents are invited to join the orientation day. For the convenience of parents,

Figure 3.4: Diversified Case Management Model

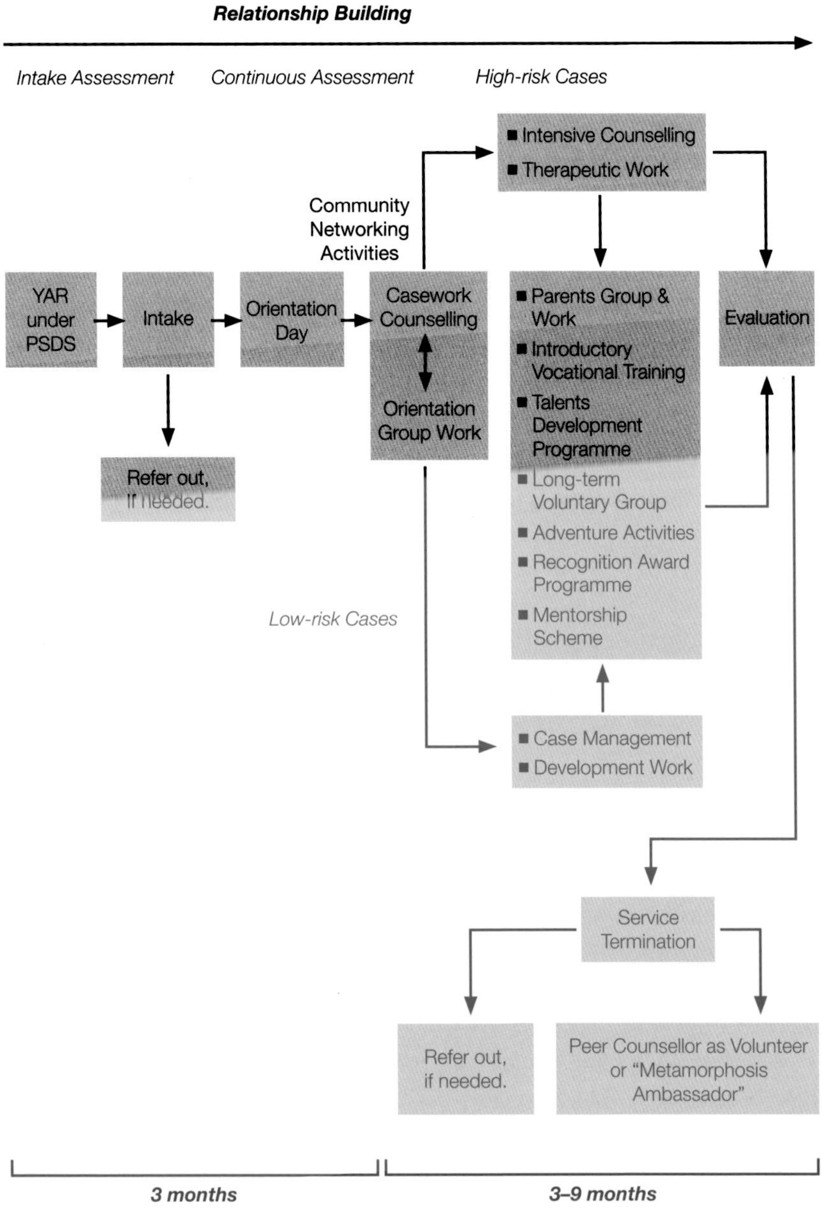

Figure 3.5: Intake Assessment Form for Cautioned YAR

Name: ______________________ *M /F Aged: ______________

Date / Intake Worker: __________________ / _________________

(*At School/ School Drop-out: since _______) (Employed / Unemployed: since _______)

I. Family

Items	Degree	Remarks
1. Relation with Parents / Family	Good / Average / Worse	
2. Follows Parents' Guidance	Willing / Average / Not Willing	
3. Parents Support Son / Daughter to Join CSSS	Supportive / Average / Not Supportive	
4. Son / Daughter Willing to Join CSSS	Active / Average / Passive	

II. Schooling / Employment

1. Academic Performance	Good / Average / Worse	
2. Conduct Behaviour	Good / Average / Worse	
3. Truancy	Never / Occasionally / Frequently	
4. Change of Job (If applicable)	Never / Occasionally / Frequently	

III. Peers, Behaviour & Others

1. Influenced by Peers	Seldom / Occasionally / Easily	
2. Stays Out till Midnight / Outside Overnight	Never / Occasionally / Frequently	
3. 1st time under PSDS	Yes / No (Previous Offence Type: _____ PSDS Date: _____)	
4. Receiving Other Social Service	Yes (Worker's Name: _____ Phone No.: _____) / No	

the orientation day is scheduled on a Sunday afternoon. During the orientation, the YAR and their parents can become known to their case workers, other CSSS social workers and the service contents of the CSSS. More importantly, the youth and their parents are invited to share their immediate service experience in person. Participants are deeply impressed by their sharing and are more willing to join those tailor-made group and community networking forthcoming activities.

Continuous assessment will be made to perceive the ACIB of the youth. The four aspects of Attachment (A), Commitment (C), Involvement (I), and Belief (B) are broken down into smaller items for assessment. This friendly assessment tool helps workers to analyse the YAR's progress. Figure 3.6 illustrates the details.

The community networking activities are enriched from time to time as more resources are mobilised to help the YAR. Parent groups/activities and mentorship scheme are two typical value added programmes in recent years. At PP, we have run two long-term parent groups, one at Eastern District and one at Southern District of Hong Kong. Parents are recruited from the orientation programmes and through the invitation of caseworkers. The parent groups serve the purpose of mutual help, and the members also contribute as "helpers" to newly joined parents. Parents share their similar experiences without shame and fear. They also grow with their children. Moreover, university students are recruited and trained as mentors for the YAR, and a one-to-one model is adopted. Positive impact has been observed for the YAR participants and their parents, and the YAR can receive an individualised academic tutoring service for free. The mentors serve as big brothers and sisters for the YAR. Other community networking activities serve other specific purposes too. One thing that is certain is that the contents of the networking activities can be extended and modified as the needs of the YAR and society change over time.

The layout of the service has to be viewed as a dynamic, instead of a static one. A social worker of PP has to make contact with the YAR and parents within five working days once the case has been assigned to him or her. An initial assessment report has to be

Figure 3.6: Continuous Assessment Form / Record for Cautioned YAR

I. Attachment: Oneself / Family / Peers / Conventional Others

Items	Degree	Remarks
1. Self-acceptance (Self-confidence)	*Accept / Improving / Refuse to Accept	
2. Emotional State	*Stable / Improving / Not Stable	
3. Parents-child / Family Relationship	*Good / Improving / Not Satisfactory	
4. Parents Support Son / Daughter to Join CSSS	*Supportive / Improving / Not Supportive	
5. Follow Parents' Guidance	*Willing / Improving / Not Willing	
6. Influenced by Undesirable Peers	*Seldom / Decreasing / Easily	
7. Relationship with Social Workers	*Good / Improving / Isolated	
8. Others:		

II. Commitment: Study / Work / Society Values and Norms

1. Academic Performance	*Good / Improving / Worse	
2. Conduct Behaviour	*Good / Improving / Worse	
3. Truancy	*Never / Decreasing / Frequently	
4. Change of Job (If applicable)	*Seldom / Decreasing / Frequently	
5. With Future Plan / Goal	*Clear / Planning / None	
6. Able to Perceive Others' Points of View	*Able / Improving / Not Able	
7. Others:		

III. Involvement: CSSS and Conventional Activities

1. Willing to Join CSSS	*Active / Improving / Passive	
2. Willing to Join Other Conventional Activities	*Active / Improving / Passive	
3. Stays Out till Midnight / Outside Overnight	*Never/ Decreasing / Frequently	
4. Undesirable / Addicted Behaviour	*Never / Decreasing / Frequently	
5. Others:		

IV. Belief: Moral Validity of Rules, Possibility of Recidivism

1. Willingness to Follow Norms, Law & Order	*High / Improving / Low	
2. Motivation to Improve / Change	*High / Improving / Low	
3. Possibility of Re-offend	*Low / Decreasing / High	
4. Others:		

**Delete whenever it applies.*

Additional Information: *Yes : ______________________________ No

V. Assessment and Intervention Plan:

( ) Strengthen Attachment of Item(s) __________ ( ) Strengthen Commitment of Item (s) __________

( ) Strengthen Involvement of Item (s) __________ ( ) Strengthen Belief of Item (s) __________

( ) Others: ______________________________

VI. Next Interview: ______________ (Date) ______________ (Time) ______________ (Venue) prepared within a one-month period. Every month, five or more cases must be brought up for supervision. For PP, every March of each year is the "review cutting line." All on-hand cases have to be updated and reviewed. This cutting line is very important as it helps the workers to organise their intervention strategies and consolidate their experiences.

User participation and worker expansion are also referred to as movable arms of the "Starfish," which facilitate and shape the service of PP into a three-dimensional one. Every YAR and his parents are involved in sharing their views and make a working contract with the social workers. Without their participation and readiness, the intervention process will be in vain. Both the YAR and the parents are "helping agents" to others too. They are invited to join as volunteers or "ambassadors" of the CSSS. Helping oneself by helping others is one of CSSS focuses that advocates the empowerment of the service users. Opinions and comments from the YAR and parents are valued and collected through the publication of service bulletins and booklets (Lo, 1998; Lo and Kam, 1994; Lo and Lee, 2006; Lo *et al.*, 2001), which helps the advancement of the service.

Just like individual YAR, each social worker is unique with special strengths and limitations. As said before, the ultimate essential elements in serving the YAR are our "heart" and commitment. Basically, the team members of CSSS must participate with that mission and vision. Then workers are encouraged to become familiar with and give feedback on the theoretical account and design of the service layout. Individual supervision, group supervision, case conferences and knowledge-sharing sessions are scheduled from time to time to facilitate learning from each other and to set up goals for expanding the helping process. To consolidate workers' practice, knowledge is also enhanced through the publication of books and bulletins. PP has published four books in the past 15 years: 1994, 1998, 2001 and 2006. The service documentation is extraordinarily worthwhile if the service maintains a mission to grow with the service users and fellow colleagues.

Community collaboration as an approach to multi-disciplinary cooperation is essential for CSSS. CSSS teams heavily depend on PSDS referrals by Police. As the personnel of the police changes frequently, CSSS teams have to update and pay visits to the new Superintendents to introduce the service and to continue building a working rapport. The Juvenile Protection Section of the Police is another crucial working partner. Regular sharing sessions and close cooperation are needed.

The rehabilitation and reintegration of the YAR within the community is one of the main themes of CSSS. CSSS will make use of every opportunity to mobilise the community to help YAR, and in return, to allow YAR to serve the community. At the case level, people around the YAR, such as parents, teachers, peers, lawyers and other support professionals are the systems that social workers in CSSS will make contact with and cooperate with for service provision. At the service level, different organisations, such as SWD, the District Council, the Fight Crime Committee, churches, NGOs, universities, commercial companies, etc., are also systems that CSSS teams must cooperate with. In addition, CSSS teams have to apply for various funding schemes, like the Community Participation Scheme, Beat Drugs Fund, AIDS Concern Fund, etc. The purpose is to mobilize more community resources for the benefit of the service.

Issue reception refers to sensible responses to issues that affect our serving targets and service directly or indirectly. We have to keep an eye on both macro and micro changes in society. The macro view includes policy, legal issues, juridical reform, socio-economic changes, etc. For example, in July 2003, the age of criminal responsibility was raised from 7 to 10. In October of the same year, the government launched Family Conference for cautioned juveniles. Family Conference (FC) is applicable when a Police Superintendent exercising the caution considers that the juvenile needs the services of three or more parties; or the juvenile is given a second or further caution (SWD and HKPF, 2003). As service providers, we have the responsibility to provide opinions and comments, and sometimes to be even more proactive by suggesting prosecution alternatives for the

Government to consider. Any legal reform or movement definitely has significant impacts on CSSS and the respective service targets.

At the micro view, we find that the characteristics of the YAR, their family composition and offence type of young people under PSDS have varied much in the past 15 years. In recent years, more YAR have become socially withdrawn and are from single parent families, while the shop-theft and theft offences also have shifted. In the past, record discs were popular theft objects, while nowadays, mobile phones and MP3s have become more popular. An increase in the proportion of young female offenders, as well as assault and sexual offences also alarm our service.

Effectiveness and Impacts of CSSS

Two systematic evaluation research projects on CSSS have been conducted: one from May 1995 till August 1996 (Lo *et al.*, 1997) and the other from July 2000 till January 2001 (Lee, 2001). The service effectiveness and positive impact of the Schemes are confirmed by the two research projects. The following briefly summarises the feedback of service users of different CSSSs.

Most YAR from CSSSs say that the services they received have helped them to become more mature and thoughtful. Their family relations and self-confidence have also been improved, and they are able to get more desirable friends. More importantly, positive behavioural changes and happier lives are reported after joining the CSSSs (Ho *et al.*, 2003; Lo and Lee, 2006). Parent service-users also say that they have witnessed positive behavioural changes in their children. Moreover, some of the parents have found an improvement in themselves, especially in respect to the relationship with their children (Lo and Lee, 2006). The prime goal of CSSSs is to help the YAR to cease offending behaviour and this result has been affirmed by related research and feedback from service recipients.

Difficulties Encountered

There are several challenges that CSSSs have encountered, as follows.

Since nearly double the manpower recourses have been pooled for each CSSS unit since August 2005, the pressure of waiting-list cases has been relieved to a great extent. But teams of CSSS have to double the number of cases to be handled. Some teams may have difficulties in securing enough case referrals during the transitional period. Much more effort has to be expended in building a firm rapport with the Police.

Good attachment with family can serve as a protective factor against YAR re-offending, but we are facing an increasing proportion of parents who are either over-protective or non-cooperative in helping their children. Workers have to adopt completely different strategies in mobilising parents' cooperation and contributions.

Though CSSSs have tried to offer the best to the YAR served, we cannot totally stop the YAR from re-offending and nor can we solve all their problems. The YAR's willingness and determination to change have important roles. There used to be a misunderstanding among workers that they may have perceived that they have done a good job for the YAR if worker-client relations are functioning under good terms. Actually, workers have to keep track of the YAR's behavioural changes, instead of only being satisfied with the good working relationship.

The change in subvention mode (i.e. Lump Sum Grant) has also limited the scope of the recruitment of workers. Most agencies tend to use the minimal wage scale to employ fresh or less experienced workers. In fact, much more time has to be expended on the training and orientation of the new recruits, as the maintenance of team stability and expertise are also challenges for CSSSs.

Striving for a good balance between service quantity and quality is another difficulty. A youngster can have different problems from time to time, but the funding body also requires case turnovers over the years. Worker need to have on-going planning concerning how far and how long he or she should offer the service.

Some people may have misconception about the YAR, especially if they have committed offences. Sometimes when we initiate the launch of a joint project with other community organisations, they may have reservations and hesitation. Some even require a pre-interview with our serving targets before agreeing to the joint venture. Although this phenomenon is not surprising, more societal education at the community level must be implemented.

Looking Beyond: Service Ahead and Conclusion

Close collaboration with the Police is a must. Instead of only maintaining the usual cooperation, regular sharing and reviewing on this joint venture are recommended. More insights could be generated by brainstorming of different professions. Moreover, the referrals of cases can be secured if positive service impact can be recognized.

In 1998, some scholars (Lo, 1998) have commented that CSSS was not keen on involving parents' participation. As time went by, all of the CSSSs have now included parents' work as one of their core tasks. Working with parents for the benefit of the YAR should continue to be a direction of CSSS work, as more and more YAR are coming from broken or complex families nowadays.

Family Conference (FC) is a new initiative aiming to bring together the cautioned YAR and their family members, professionals from relevant Government departments and NGOs to assess the needs of the cautioned juveniles and to draw up a follow-up plan to address the identified juvenile's needs through their joint efforts. According to a review, this initiative has received positive results (SWD, 2005), but the operation system has to be further strengthened. For example, now only the Police Superintendent has the right to assess whether criteria for calling FC are met. It has been suggested that both Police and social workers of CSSSs should have the right to consider and recommend to SWD the calling of a FC. Moreover, the FC evaluation committee should not be composed only of operation units, i.e. SWD, Police, related NGOs, Education and Manpower Bureau (then), but also of policy-making units, i.e. Security Bureau and Department of Justice, so that FC can be improved both in practical ways and at the legislative level.

FC and PSDS are sometimes criticised as only looking at the "welfare and opportunity" of the cautioned juveniles, without holding the juveniles accountable and responsible for their offending behaviour. "Compensation/repairing" elements are included in PP's counselling service and community networking activities. According to our experience, it is very therapeutic and significant to the cautioned youth if they can have opportunities to repair or compensate for their wrong-doings. "Immediate and frequent intervention" is an effective buffer for YAR to prevent recidivism. More working strategies have to be identified.

Some Western countries, e.g. the Queensland Department of Justice in Australia, have initiated amendments to their juvenile justice acts and incorporated the practice of restorative justice processes when dealing with juvenile delinquents. The element of victim participation is important, because it allows the cautioned youth and victims to speak, to express and have a say in the outcomes. But in Hong Kong, victim participation is still not a common practice. The Government is now considering the pros and cons of introducing victim participation into the existing measures, and the authors believe that it should be further concretized and implemented. It may be that those PSDS cases are a good testing ground for the "victim-offender mediation" (VOM) or "Youth Justice Conferencing" (YJC) measure in Hong Kong.

To conclude, the authors will end this chapter with the following story:

> *The sea tides flood and ebb every day, and hundreds of starfishes remain on the beaches when the tides go out. A wise old man helps to save the starfishes and throws them back into the sea one by one each day. People think that he is wasting time, but he insists on doing the same action with the mission that, even though he cannot save all lives, he values the fact that he can save some.*

CSSSs cannot stop all YAR from offending/re-offending, but they are helping the YAR just like the wise old man. The "Starfish Wisdom" reminds us of the core mission of CSSSs.

References

Aguilera, D. C. and Messick, J. M. (1987). *Crisis Intervention: Theory and Methodology*. St. Louis: The C. V. Mosby Company.

Chief Executive (2000). *The 2000 Policy Address*. Hong Kong: Government Printer.

Cheung, Y. W. (1993). *Predicting Adolescent Deviant Behavior in Hong Kong: A Comparison of Media, Family, School and Peer Variables*. Hong Kong: Hong Kong Institute of Asia-Pacific Studies, The Chinese University of Hong Kong.

Cheung, Y. W. and Ng, A. (1988). "Social Factors in Adolescent Deviant Behavior in Hong Kong: An Integrated Theoretical Approach," *International Journal of Comparative and Applied Criminal Justice, Volume 12*, pp. 27–45.

Elliott, D. S., Huizinga, D., and Ageton, S. S. (1985). *Explaining Delinquency and Drug Use*. Beverly Hill: Sage.

Fight Crime Committee (1996). *1996 Report of Fight Crime Committee*. Hong Kong: Government Printer.

Golan, N. (1978). *Treatment in Crisis Situation*. New York: Free Press.

Hong Kong Federation of Youth Groups (1993). *Decriminalizing Juvenile Offences: Police Superintendents' Discretion Scheme and*

Follow-up Services. (Youth Study Series No. 2) Hong Kong: Hong Kong Federation of Youth Groups.

Hirschi, T. (1969). *Causes of Delinquency.* Los Angeles: University of California Press.

Jang, S. J., and Smith, C. A. (1997). "A Test of Reciprocal Causal Relationships among Parental Supervision, Affective Ties, and Delinquency," *Journal of Research in Crime and Delinquency, Volume 34,* pp. 307–336.

Krohn, N. D., Lizotte, A. J., Thornberry, T. P., Smith, C. A., and McDowall, D. (1996). "Reciprocal Causal Relationships among Drug Use, Peers, and Beliefs: A Five-wave Panel Model," *Journal of Drug Issues, Volume 26,* pp. 405–428.

Lam, D. O. P. (1998). "Social Causes of Juvenile Crime," *Journal of Youth Studies, Volume 1 (2),* pp. 1–9. Hong Kong: The Hong Kong Federation of Youth Groups.

Lee, F. W. L. (1996). *Teens of the Night: A Study on Night Drifting Young People in Hong Kong.* Hong Kong: The Chinese University of Hong Kong.

Lee, F. W. L. (2005). *Working with Youth-at-Risk in Hong Kong.* Hong Kong: Hong Kong University Press.

Lee, K. M. (2001). *The Impacts of Community Support Service Scheme on Young Offenders: A Case Study of Project Phoenix.* (Unpublished M.Soc.Sc. Dissertation) Hong Kong: The University of Hong Kong.

Lo, T. W., Wong S. W, Chan W. T., Leung S. K., Yu, C. S., and Chan, C. K. (1997). *Research on the Effectiveness of Rehabilitation Programmes for Young Offenders: Full Report.* Hong Kong: City University of Hong Kong.

Ng, A. M. C., Lau, T. S., Lu, A., Tsoi, R. and Wong, K. H. (1975). *Social Causes of Violent Crimes among Young Offenders in Hong Kong.* Hong Kong: Social Research Centre, The Chinese University of Hong Kong.

Ng, A. M. C. (1980). *Family Relationships and Delinquent Behavior.* Columbia: Columbia University.

Ng, A. M. C. (1994). "Delinquency Trends in Socio-economic Perspective," In *Twenty-five Years of Social and Economic Development in Hong Kong,* edited by B. K. P. Leung, B. K. P. and T. Y. C. Wong, pp. 357–

378. Hong Kong: Centre of Asian Studies, The University of Hong Kong.

Parad, H. (1971). "Crisis Intervention," In *Encyclopedia of Social Work,* (16th edition), edited by R. Morris, pp. 196–202. New York: National Association of Social Workers.

Parry, G. (1990). *Problems in Practice: Coping with Crisis.* London: Routledge.

Roberts, A. (2000). "An Overview of Crisis Theory and Crisis Intervention," In *Crisis Intervention Handbook: Assessment, Treatment, Research,* edited by A. Roberts, pp. 3–29. New York: Oxford University Press.

Social Welfare Department (1973). *The Five Year Plan for Social Welfare Development in Hong Kong, 1973–1978.* Hong Kong: Government Printer.

Social Welfare Department (2005). *Summary of the Review Report on Family Conference.* Hong Kong: Government Printer.

Social Welfare Department and Hong Kong Police Force. (2003). *Protocol on Conducting Family Conference for Children/Juveniles Cautioned under the Police Superintendent's Discretion Scheme.* Hong Kong: Youth and Corrections Section, SWD and Child Protection Policy Unit, HK Police Force.

Thornberry, T. P. (1987). "Toward an Interactional Theory of Delinquency," *Criminology, Volume 25 (4),* pp. 863–891.

Thornberry, T. P., Lizotte, A. J., Krohn, M. D., Farnworth, M., and Jang, S. J. (1991). "Testing Interactional Theory: An Examination of Reciprocal Causal Relationships among Family, School, and Delinquency," *Journal of Criminal Law and Criminology, Volume 82 (1),* pp. 3–35.

Trojanowicz, R. C., and Morash, M. (1992). *Juvenile Delinquency: Concepts and Control.* (5th ed.) Englewood Cliffs, NJ: Prentice Hall.

Vagg, J., Bacon-Shone, J., Gray, P., and Lam, D., (1995). *The Social Causes of Juvenile Crime.* Hong Kong: University of Hong Kong.

Weis, J. G., Crutchfield, R. D., and Bridges, G. S., (1996). *Juvenile Delinquency of Crime and Society.* (Volume 2) New York: Pine Forge Press.

Working Group (1994). *Report on Review of the Superintendents' Discretion Scheme*. Hong Kong: Government Printer.

Working Party (1994). *Report on Review of Children and Youth Centre Services*. Hong Kong: Working Party on Review of Children and Youth Centre Services.

黃成榮、李永年及盧鐵榮（1995）。《屯門區青少年行為問題研究：剖析青少年步向越軌青少年的新取向》。香港：屯門區議會出版。

黃成榮（1997）。《危機青少年之越軌過程：個案追蹤研究報告》。香港：基督教信義會北區外展社會工作隊。

黃成榮（1999）。《青少年價值觀及違規行為探索》。香港：三聯書店。

盧錦華、金明（1994）。《火鳳凰——再生的故事》。香港：循道衛理書室。

盧錦華（1998）。《鳳凰展翅——社區支援服務文集》。香港：循道衛理書室。

盧錦華、李冠美、呂慧敏（2001）。《展翅上騰——探索先導青少年服務新路向》。香港：循道衛理書室。

盧錦華、李冠美（2006）。《「挫」中「福」集——青少年蛻變實錄》。香港： 循道衛理中心。

何琴、黃志慧、盧淑馨（2003）。《青少年自強計劃02–03年度工作報告》。基督教香港信義會。

循道衛理中心（2006）。《火鳳凰——社區支援服務計劃》單張。

香港遊樂場協會（2006）。《新境界——社區支援服務計劃》單張。

基督教香港信義會（2006）。《青少年自強計劃YES透視生命色彩》單張。

香港青年協會（2004）。《青年支援服務計劃》單張。

香港小童群益會（2006）。《青鋒網——社區支援服務計劃》單張。

POLICE SCHOOL LIAISON SCHEME

4

Francis Wing-lin LEE

Background

The Police School Liaison Scheme (PSLS), which was launched in 1974, has more than 30 years of history. In fact, it was developed according to the concept of community policing which was quite popular in the 1970s (Fielding, 1995; Miller and Hess, 1998 and 2005; Oliver, 2000; Schaffer, 1980; Trojanowicz *et al.*, 1998). This concept basically says that if the police have developed a harmonious relationship with the community, this would facilitate their crime-fighting and prevention work. With this philosophy as the back-up framework, different strategies have been developed by the police forces in different countries to foster a good and harmonious relationship with the communities they are responsible for. With this concept in mind, the PSLS in Hong Kong was developed as a part of the strategies to develop a cooperative relationship with schools (primary and secondary), and for detection and prevention of juvenile crime.

Under this Scheme, dedicated police officers were appointed as School Liaison Officers (SLOs) to keep a close liaison with schools they were responsible for, to provide various relevant advice, and to organise various related activities for the schools. With the inception of the Neighbourhood Police Coordination Scheme in 1984, the SLOs also needed to assume the role of Neighbourhood Police Coordinators for building up good community relations (www.info.gov.hk/police/hkp-home/english/pprb/schlia/slossloprg.htm).

As the juvenile crime problem was gradually increasing in the 1980s and had attracted much public concern, in August 1988, 26 SLO posts were re-established. "As part of a comprehensive programme of support services for youth at risk, 33 Secondary School Liaison Officer (SSLO) posts at sergeant rank were created in August 2001 to strengthen police commitment in juvenile crime prevention work."

According to the related official website of the Force (www.info.gov.hk/police/hkp-home/english/pprb/schlia/slossloprg.htm), the objectives of the PSLS are:

(a) to establish a good relationship between the police and the school community—children, teachers and parents;

(b) on the basis of this relationship, to give schoolchildren an understanding of the role of the police and a respect for law and order;

(c) to make schoolchildren aware of various dangers which they may encounter, such as the dangers of involvement in crime, drug abuse, Triad association, hooliganism, sexual temptations and abuse, and road traffic, etc.;

(d) to alert schoolchildren and school authorities to the need for crime prevention in all its aspects;

(e) to instil a sense of discipline and positive values in schoolchildren at risk, through group or individual discussions with them;

(f) to refer suitable cases to the relevant multi-agency programme for follow-up action, in consultation with the social workers, school management and parents; and

(g) to act as the focal point of contact on behalf of the Police Community Relations Officer between local Police and the District Social Welfare Office, as well as the school management.

Roles of SLOs/SSLOs

All newly appointed and potential SLOs/SSLOs have to attend a training programme (School Support Liaison Course) of 6.5 days organised by the Police Public Relations Bureau (PPRB).

Recognising that a good working relationship between the school community (e.g. principals, teachers, school social workers, students, etc.) and police is important for the success of the PSLS, responsible police are to help schools "to instil a sense of responsibility, moral values and personal discipline" into their students. The stated main roles of the SLOs/SSLOs include:

(a) advise school management on the enforcement of the law in regard to unruly behaviour of students in the school;

(b) conduct group/individual discussion with school children at risk, to instil a sense of discipline and positive values in them;

(c) after discussion with the school management and parents, refer suitable cases to the relevant multi-agency programme for follow-up action; and

(d) give lectures on crime related topics including drugs, Triads and other relevant issues to strengthen students' awareness of various crimes, with a view to preventing them from falling prey to bad elements.

Programme Contents

Depending on the unique situations and creativity of responsible police in different communities, various related strategies are developed in order to actualise the aims of PSLS and roles of the SLOs/SSLOs. Holding school talks with students, teachers and parents on different related topics; running workshops for teachers; advising school management on the handling of unruly students and school order or security issues; interviewing unruly students, etc. are basic tasks that the SLOs/SSLOs need to do in performing their roles.

From the Police Community Relations Officers' Manual (PPRB, n.d.), the practices of PSLS are suggested. They include:

(a) formal lectures to target groups;

(b) discussions with groups or individuals either formally in the classroom or at random in the school halls and on the grounds;

(c) case studies;

(d) special project publicity;

(e) informal visits by patrol officers;

(f) organising/participating/supporting sporting, social and outdoor pursuits;

(g) arranging visits to police stations, other police establishments (e.g. PTS) and police social functions (e.g. Beating Retreat);

(h) organising JPC school clubs;

(i) developing recreational activities with fighting crime or educational/character developmental themes; and

(j) exhibitions.

One of the police districts, which has a good reputation in doing school liaison work, is Tuen Mun Police District. Besides carrying out those above-mentioned basic tasks, under the guidance and supervision of the Police Community Relations Office of the District, they also periodically issue newsletters on different district matters concerning juveniles (e.g. the juvenile crime situation, reminders for vacation, activities of children and youth centres, crime reporting, etc.). A webpage on youth crime information has also been established to advise young people on how to avoid different kinds of crime/unruly behaviour, e.g. bullying, computer crime, Triad activities, etc. A webpage titled "Youth Activities" has also been designed to have a crossword puzzle, and to publicize different youth activities organised in the District (www.ln.edu.hk/tmpol-schnet/toppage.htm).

Challenges

Through cooperating with some school personnel (e.g. principals and senior teachers), it is observed that, although the aims of the PSLS are good, it has encountered some challenges.

Perceived Function of the Scheme

As the public image of Police is crime fighting, although the aims of the Scheme are multiple (i.e. not only crime fighting), it would be understandable that many school personnel see the Scheme as a crime-fighting strategy. This perceived function of the Scheme presents challenges to the local police, especially those responsible for SLOs/SSLOs, in their effort to work with the schools under the Scheme since the schools might feel being labelled as "problematic" or "bad" if they are approached by responsible SLOs/SSLOs. This perceived stigmatisation is especially strong for those upper-banding schools that may usually resolve or handle conflicts within schools by themselves, avoiding contact with police. This is a common challenge that the PSLS has faced.

Cooperation of Schools

With the above-mentioned perceived function of the Scheme, it would be difficult to get genuine and full cooperation from schools for the work of the responsible SLOs/SSLOs. In order to present a "friendly" image, schools may invite SLOs/SSLOs in their districts to conduct talks to their students in assembles. But for real and hard-core cases, which should be the expertise of police, the schools may try to resolve or handle those cases by themselves first. This kind of mentality is not only common for school principals, but also for teachers. If the schools' intervention could not resolve or handle the problems, intervention by the police would be called for. In order to maintain the reputation of the schools, the call for police intervention would be a last resort. However, at this stage, the intervention of the police would not be at the level of the SLO/SSLOs, but would most likely be the Criminal Investigation Department (CID) whose investigation procedure may be "less friendly."

Expertise of SLOs/SSLOs

Although there are some roles and responsibilities that have been mentioned as the jobs of SLOs/SSLOs, they may not be inclusive. The responsible SLOs/SSLOs may find difficulties in advising on issues which commonly happen in schools, but which fall outside the expertise of the SLOs/SSLOs. One such example is bullying (without a Triad connection). Even the responsible SLOs/SSLOs may try their best to advise on the handling of the issues, but their opinions may not be appropriate and helpful, and may not be adopted. External experts (non-police) may be invited to give advice, which may reduce the perceived helpfulness of the SLOs/SSLOs. Moreover, for issues which may be police-related (e.g. selling of dangerous drugs (DD) at schools), police from the relevant squad might be invited to give advice or take action. This further reduces the credential of the SLOs/SSLOs and, in this case, the credit would be given to the police as a whole, but not to the responsible SLOs/SLOs.

Impacts of Local and Other Conditions

In fact, all the above-mentioned challenges to PSLS depend much on the conditions of the districts where the schools are located. For example, if the extent of delinquent behaviour of young people (students) in the districts where the schools are situated is low, then the cooperation of the schools with the responsible SLOs/SSLOs would not be high, while the opposite would also be true but would put much pressure on the performance of the responsible SLOs/SSLOs. If the school personnel are quite eager to retain the good reputation of the schools and do not welcome police presence in the schools, the work of the responsible SLOs/SSLOs would not be easy to carry out.

As stated in Chapter 5 on *Police School Liaison of Police Community Relations Officers' Manual* (PPRB, n.d.), "(t)he SLO/SSLO will maintain regular contact with officers of the District School Support Team (DATS) to coordinate school liaison, and activities in a concerted approach to achieve optimal effect and productivity."

Way Forward?

As stated by a responsible officer of the PPRB, there is no particular plan for the future development of the Scheme at this stage, but they will certainly monitor the progress of its daily operation, such as through the monthly Secondary School Liaison Officers' Meeting, and will review the Scheme whenever there is a need.

The PSLS is one of a few proactive interventions, launched in the 1970s, which is carried out by the Police for preventing juvenile crime, and has a history of more than 30 years. Obviously with such a long history, reviewing and planning for future development are necessary. Although the image of the Hong Kong Police Force is rather reactive (i.e. passively responding to the committing of crimes), this Scheme helps to promote a proactive image of the Police, at least for juvenile crime. The further strengthening and promotion of this Scheme may be necessary strategies to convey a proactive image of the Police to the public.

Acknowledgements

The provision of relevant materials from the Police Public Relations Bureau for writing up this chapter must be acknowledged.

References

Commissioner of Police (2005). *Hong Kong Police Force—2004 Review.* Hong Kong: Government Printer.

Fielding, N. (1995). *Community Policing.* Oxford: Clarendon Press.

Hong Kong Police Force (various years) www.info.gov.hk/police/hkp-home/english/index.htm

Miller, L. S. and Hess, K. M. (1998). *The Police in the Community: Strategies for the 21st Century.* (2nd edition) Belmont, CA: West/Wadsworth.

Miller, L. S. and Hess, K. M. (2005). *Community Policing: Partnerships for Problem Solving.* (4th edition) Australia: Thomson

Oliver, W. M. (ed.) (2000). *Community Policing: Classical Readings.* Upper Saddle River, NJ: Prentice Hall.

Police Public Relations Bureau (PPRB) (n.d.). *Police Community Relations Officers' Manual.* (Chapter 5: Police School Liaison) (The Police Intranet) (for internal reference).

Police School Liaison Scheme. (www.info.gov.hk/police/hkp-home/english/pprb/schlia/ slossloprg.htm)

Schaffer, E. B. (1980). *Community Policing.* London: Croom Helm.

Trojanowicz, R. *et al.* (1998). *Community Policing: A Contemporary Perspective.* (2/e) Cincinnati, OH: Anderson Publications. (www.ln.edu.hk/tmpol-schnet/toppage.htm)

5

HOTLINE SERVICE FOR YOUTH-AT-RISK

Siu-man HSU

Introduction

Hotline services are not new for Hong Kong people. According to the statistical report of the Hong Kong Council of Social Service in 2005, there are more than 270 hotline services provided by over 150 non-governmental organisations (NGOs). Though hotline services are not a mainstream mode of counselling compared to face-to-face or group counselling, they are a very convenient and accessible channel of communication and are widely adopted as a service mode in many settings. In this chapter, we will review the development and characteristics of hotline services for young people in Hong Kong, especially for youth-at-risk. The impact of the service will also be discussed.

It would be difficult to define concretely who "youth-at-risk" are (Capuzzi and Gross, 1996; Dryfoos, 1998; Ungar, 2006), but it is believed that the young callers who use the hotline service are "at-risk" and in need of immediate help of some kind, as otherwise they would not have called the hotline. Therefore, the young callers who use the hotline service are regarded as "at-risk" youth.

What is Telephone or Hotline Counselling?

Telephone or hotline counselling is defined as a service whereby a trained counsellor works with a client, or a group of clients, by telephone, to enable the client(s) to explore personal situation(s), problems or crises either in a one-off or a longer-term therapeutic relationship (Rosenfield, 1997). Telephone counselling was first used widely in the 1960s by suicide prevention and crisis intervention services as a means of providing immediate and inexpensive access to crisis intervention for those in distress.

According to Rosenfield (1997), there are several functions for offering counselling by phone, such as advice-giving, advocacy, information-giving, support and befriending. Telephone has been used as a means of counselling in a variety of services (Lester and Brockopp, 2002), including suicide prevention centres, crisis intervention centres, youth hotlines, rape crisis counselling centres, drug hotlines, parents' hotlines, and sex information.

Hotline Service for Young People

Young people tend to be reluctant to seek counselling services as compared to other age groups. Young people may feel "faceless" when they need to go to see a counsellor or social worker. The situation is more obvious in school and residential settings as youngsters do not want to admit their problems among their fellow students or inmates. Young people are less motivated to have counselling sessions even if they are invited to do so. However, hotline services are characterised by their anonymous nature because callers do not need to reveal their identities. This may diminish the "labelling effect" of face-to face counselling.

Furthermore, young people like to communicate with their peers by telephone and through the internet. In the 1980s, it was common and popular for young people to spend long hours on the phone talking to their friends. In this decade, online and mobile phone chatting have become trendy means of communication among young people. Personalised telecommunications enable people to know and send ideas and thoughts at high speed. But hotline or telephone counselling still provides a cost-effective way to reach professionals and obtain advice. Young people may find the telephone a comfortable medium through which to express their inner feelings and distress, and counsellors cannot identify them through the calls. In fact, counselling via telephone has a number of important benefits as outlined below.

First, immediacy of service provision is a distinct feature, particularly in respect to information, referral and crisis counselling services. The telephone enables the provision of counselling to individuals when they need it, whether in crisis or not. Due to the anonymous nature of a hotline, it enables increased client access to services. Clients are able to access services from the comfort of their own home, work, or anywhere that they have access to telephones. The major benefit of telephone counselling is that those who are normally deprived of professional services are able to access the services with minimal disruption of their daily lives.

Second, anonymity could lower the risk for a client who is afraid of face-to-face counselling. The telephone can allow a caller to talk to a counsellor without being seen and to remain somewhat unknown. As the counsellor cannot see the physical signs of the client, the client's feeling of inferiority may be reduced. It may prevent the client from feeling weak or incompetent because of seeking help. It also enables him/her to be more expressive as it allows the caller to feel safe from the shame or embarrassment that he/she may imagine occurring in a face-to-face setting.

The sense of control by clients is another attraction of telephone counselling, as communication over the telephone may help them feel that they have more control over the process of counselling. They may feel more comfortable because of the relative ease with which they can terminate the telephone sessions if they wish to do so. It is much easier to simply hang up a telephone than it is to walk out of an interviewing room.

The advantage of perceived control is considered important for group counselling, especially for adolescent groups, who may be sensitive to the issue. The use of telephone counselling may be an effective way of establishing a therapeutic alliance with callers. Through years of experience, it is believed that the positive experience of telephone counselling of callers, especially young people, may facilitate a transition to face-to-face counselling.

All the above stated advantages of a hotline have made its services attractive to young people, especially the youth-at-risk who may frequently experience problems and want to have someone to talk to.

Development of "Youthline" of Hong Kong Federation of Youth Groups (HKFYG)

Hotline services provided by government departments and NGOs give immediate information and consultations to the general public. The first such service in Hong Kong was set up in the 1960s by the Samaritan Befriender to provide support for those considering suicide. The suicide prevention hotline was manned and operated by trained volunteers 24 hours a day, 7 days a week, territory-wide for callers of all ages.

To cope with the increasing needs of young people for counselling services, the Hong Kong Federation of Youth Groups set up a pilot youth counselling service in 1971. Youthline (2777-8899) was established in 1993 with the support of the Hong Kong Jockey Club Charities Trust in response to a spate of adolescent suicide cases. The Social Welfare Department began to subvent Youthline in 1995 as a result of favourable responses from youths to the hotline.

In a pledge made by the Social Welfare Department in 1995:

> *Hotline service for youth at risk is to support young people through telephone contact by offering help in an easy and convenient way in crisis situation without exposing their identities, facilitating them to solve their own problems and providing counselling service which can help them ease their distress.*

In the same year, a 24-hour free Infoline service, sponsored by the Cable and Wireless Hong Kong Telecom, was launched by the HKFYG. The objective was to ease the demand on Youthline by helping callers to master skills to solve their daily problems themselves. Although this sponsorship ended in 1999, the Infoline service was resumed in the HKFYG in September 2002 with the support from the Sir McLehose Trust Fund. It continues to provide counselling messages via tailor-made stories, current tips and information when calls are transferred to the service because counsellors are occupied with other callers.

To meet the needs of young people, Youthline was extended to 24 telephone lines manned by trained social workers in 2002. It operates from Monday to Saturday, 12 hours a day from 2 p.m. to 2 a.m. Cases of deep-rooted problems are referred for face-to-face counselling by the Youth Counselling Centre of the Federation or other related services of some NGOs.

Service Objectives of Youthline

The objectives of the service are:

(a) to provide immediate support to young people in crisis and distress, so that they may tackle their problems in positive ways;

(b) to help young people improve and consolidate their coping abilities to assist them in facing challenges at a young age;

(c) to help young people acquire greater maturity by promoting their self-awareness and developing their potential; and

(d) to promote youth counselling services to the public and encourage them to seek help when needed.

Service Contents of Youthline

At present, Youthline offers telephone as well as face-to-face counselling to young people who are in need of immediate intervention or further referrals. Counselling services provided through email and internet are also provided. On the average, Youthline has about 50,000 incoming calls per month and the average number of cases handled each month are approximately 4,000. This huge demand for hotline services shows that "at-risk" young people are looking for convenient and immediate ways to handle their stress and emotions. To ease the great demand on Youthline, the 24-hour free Infoline service to hotline callers came into play. Tailor-made and up-to-date information are provided to young callers who are not immediately able to get access to hotline counsellors. On the average, over 300,000 callers access to Infoline per annum. If they are unable to reach counsellors on the phone, they are encouraged to leave voice messages for follow-up service.

Youthline offers immediate emotional support to young people in crisis. During the SARS outbreak in 2003, the role and functions of the hotline services were obvious. During that time, many young people were frustrated, bored and in low spirits and all schools were closed. The hotline service was extended from 10 a.m. to 2 a.m. and many new items, including health tips, storytelling and current news reporting were introduced. The hotline service became one of the safest and most effective means for youth to express their concerns and emotions. From late March to mid-May 2003, Youthline recorded over a million incoming calls, and hotline counsellors and the Infoline service provided immediate support for over 249,000 callers. This shows that hotline counselling can fill a territory-wide need for supportive services to young people.

In December 2004, the tragedy of the Asian Tsunami affected adversely the mood of many people in Hong Kong. The hotline service had offered support to youngsters who felt emotionally disturbed by the incident. A series of hot-tips were prepared for parents, young people and teachers on how to handle fear and unstable emotions.

In line with the current trend of increased communication through the internet, Youthline began online counselling service via email, ICQ and MSN from 2001 onwards. In collaboration with websites such as Hong Kong Education City, Mingpao Life, Sina and Yahoo, it offers young people a convenient way to post their enquiries and questions. Quick and accurate responses from counsellors are then given. During the period of the release of public examination results, instant communication, such as MSN and ICQ, is a very popular means for students to seek help and information.

Some Implications

An Extension of Conventional Counselling Service

In traditional social work training, social workers are mainly taught how to offer face-to-face counselling. However, telephone counselling is not a main focus of teaching and it is quite different from face-to-face counselling because workers need to be prompt in venting and calming callers' emotions and helping them to air their problems. The hotline counsellor must make a quick assessment and formulate an appropriate intervention plan. Hotline counselling can be regarded as an extension of conventional face-to-face counselling service. It is anonymous and convenient and fits young people's need to seek immediate help. Most importantly, it offers callers, especially young people, a sense of security. From our experience, we find that many of our callers prefer to contact the counsellors by telephone because they feel more comfortable in disclosing their problems to counsellors through the phone.

Long and Consistent Service Hours

Youthline operates six days a week from Monday to Saturday including public holidays, 12 hours a day, from 2 p.m. to 2 a.m. These long service hours mean that immediate help is available even when young people are out of school or work. Given the popularity of mobile phones and internet services, they can reach hotline counsellors to seek advice anywhere and anytime. Hotline counsellors sometimes received calls from young night drifters and youth-at-risk who are still out at midnight. Prompt responses and help, and appropriate referrals are made instantly. Long and consistent service hours enable callers to receive proper counselling support even after office hours.

Expertise in Handling Crises and Short-term Cases

Youthline counsellors together usually handle an average of 147 calls each day and they have rich experience in tackling different problems of various kinds. This hones the skills and knowledge of the counsellors (social workers) and they become increasingly familiar with the community resources. In emergent situations, hotline services provide instant contact. For example, when a caller has suicidal thoughts, a hotline counsellor can help him to vent his emotions and assess the risk levels. The seeking of other counsellors' assistance and mobilising appropriate community resources such as police, out-reach services or temporary shelter are quite common in the service. Moreover, when waiting for referrals to other services or agencies, hotline counsellors can set short-term goals with the callers and prepare them for the new service settings.

Conclusion

Hotlines are adopted as a means of providing crisis services for "youth-at-risk" in Hong Kong. With their strengths, accessibility, anonymity and capacity to offer clients a sense of control and security, they have become efficient and cost-effective service channels. Because of the reluctance of young people, especially "youth-at-risk," to reveal and admit their problems for fear of losing face, hotline services offer a way out because they do not need to identify themselves until they are ready to do so. By enhancing the self-awareness of young callers and helping them cope with changes, hotlines can help them become more confident to tackle the problems they encounter and to face new challenges.

References

Capuzzi, D. and Gross, D. R. (eds.) (1996). *Youth at Risk: A Preventive Resource for Counselors, Teachers, and Parents.* (2nd edition). Alexandria, VA: American Counseling Association.

Coman, G. J., Burrows, G. D., Evans, B. J. (2001). "Telephone Counselling in Australia: Application and Considerations for Use." *British Journal of Guidance and Counselling, Volume.29(2),* pp. 247–258.

Dryfoos, J. G. (1998). *Safe Passage: Making it through Adolescence in a Risky Society.* Oxford: Oxford University Press.

Lester, D. and Brockopp, G. W. (2002). *Crisis Intervention and Counselling by Telephone.* Springfield: Charles C Thomas.

Rosenfield, M. (1997). *Counselling by Telephone.* London: Sage.

Ungar, M. (2006). *Strengths-based Counseling with At-risk Youth.* California: Corwin Press.

COUNSELLING CENTRE FOR YOUNG PSYCHOTROPIC SUBSTANCE ABUSERS

6

Siu-ming TO and Benson Kwok-kai CHAN

Introduction

This chapter examines the current development of counselling centres' services for young substance abusers and the field experiences of practitioners in adopting an existential approach to intervention and prevention. Substance abuse has long been a social problem in Hong Kong. The incidence of substance abuse has been characterised by the predominance of heroin addiction before the late 1980s (Cheung and Cheung, 2006). However, in recent years the popularity of heroin has become obsolete due to the rising trend of psychotropic substance abuse among young people. The number of reported psychotropic substance abusers has steadily increased from 2,238 in 1994 to 3,493 in 1999 (Narcotics Division, 2003). Its rapid spread might be associated with the prevalence of rave parties and discos in the late 1990s (Lam *et al.*, 2004; Ngai *et al.*, 2006). The problem of cross-boundary substance abuse also brings new challenges due to the lower price of drugs and easier drug distribution in the mainland (Chan and Chung, in press; Lau, 2003). The most popular substances abused by adolescents include Ecstasy, Ketamine, Cannabis, and Amphetamine (Narcotics Division, 2007). More attention has been paid to the escalating misuse of Ketamine and Ecstasy. The proportion of Ketamine abuse rose from 0.1% in 1997 to 72.8% in 2002, while Ecstasy abuse rose from 2.3% to 35.9% in the same period (Narcotics Division, 2006). It becomes clear that the government, police, social workers, educators, parents, and community members need to play their respective roles in assuaging the problem.

Development of Counselling Centres for Young Substance Abusers in Hong Kong

From Institution-orientation to Community-orientation

In the past, the government adopted a multi-modality approach in providing treatment and rehabilitation services for substance abusers.

These include the compulsory placement scheme, the voluntary out-patient methadone treatment programme, and the voluntary out-patient programme run by non-governmental organisations and Christian therapeutic agencies (Narcotics Division, 2006). These services tended to be institution-orientated rather than community-orientated, and they were mainly designed to help heroin addicts. An institution-orientated approach is beneficial for rehabilitation because addicts must experience strong withdrawal symptoms, both physically and psychologically. However, it may not be the most effective way to help psychotropic substance abusers, as there is a trend that most of them take illicit drugs for recreational and social purposes.

The rising rate of psychotropic substance abuse in the 1990s has aroused a lot of public concern, which sparked the government's commitment to providing additional resources to suit the various needs of drug takers. Three counselling centres for psychotropic substance abusers (CCPSAs) were thus established in different districts in the late 1990s, namely the Caritas HUGS Centre in New Territories West, Hong Kong Christian Service PS33 in Kowloon West, and Hong Kong Lutheran Social Service Cheer Lutheran Centre in New Territories East. These centres used a community-based approach in delivering individual and group counselling services to drug abusers, as well as organizing various prevention programmes.

From Fragmented Service to One-stop Service

The seriousness of substance abuse and the changing mode of drug use in the early 2000s brought about a shortage of manpower and a heavy workload among the existing CCPSAs. In order to meet the service demand and achieve the full coverage of therapeutic and rehabilitation services for psychotropic substance abusers, two more CCPSAs were set up, one in Hong Kong Island run by the Tung Wah Hospitals Groups CROSS Centre and one in Kowloon East run by the Hong Kong Lutheran Social Service Evergreen

Lutheran Centre, respectively. The total number of CCPSAs was thus expanded from three to five. Meanwhile, the Against Substance Abuse Scheme operated by the Social Welfare Department, which organised community-based prevention programmes for occasional abusers, was terminated in 2002. The resources were reallocated to the CCPSAs with a view to strengthening the drug prevention programmes for secondary school students, as well as offering more accessible services and early interventions to potential drug users.

To offer one-stop service and strengthen the collaboration with other non-governmental organisations, the CCPSAs were granted additional resources to provide outreaching service in 2008. It is expected that they will build coalitions with the District Youth Outreaching Social Work Teams and the Overnight Outreaching Services to visit black spots and approach youth aged below 21. Indeed, the setting up of CCPSAs helps with pooling different resources and targeting young drug abusers in a comprehensive manner. They gain varied experience in offering counselling services, drug prevention programmes, and outreaching services, as well as training programmes for other youth workers. These experiences are important to the development of an integrated, multidimensional, dynamic, and strategic model for effective substance abuse counselling and education. In the future, two additional CCPSAs will be established to serve different communities (Narcotic Division, 2008).

Service Operation of Counselling Centres for Young Substance Abusers

At present, there are five CCPSAs providing treatment and rehabilitation services to psychotropic substance abusers. Although these centres adopt different working approaches, they all provide non-residential services for young drug addicts (Narcotics Division, 2007). Types of major services include:

Rehabilitative services for helping young substance abusers to abstain from drug-taking habits and encouraging them to develop healthy lifestyles and to achieve positive development, which includes assessment, matching modes of detoxification, relapse prevention, and individual and group counselling.

Preventive education programmes are launched to secondary school students so as to enhance their awareness of the harmful effects of drug misuse. Those students who are potential or occasional substance abusers are identified, and receive a series of follow-up services, such as workshops and groups. If necessary, individual counselling is given to help them relinquish their drug-taking behaviour and regain their confidence in school life.

Counselling services and supportive programmes for helping family members of substance abusers in the course of treatment and rehabilitation, which comprise individual and family counselling, parent mutual support groups, and parent education programmes.

Outreaching services provide help for young people aged below 21, who are hanging out in black spots under undesirable peer influences. Practitioners establish close ties with other youth service providers in the community in response to their common concerns over young substance abusers.

Training programmes for related professionals to prepare them to work with potential, occasional, and habitual substance abusers. Consultations and inquiries are also offered to persons or agencies in need.

As mentioned above, the CCPSAs were set up by pooling various resources to provide a one-stop service for psychotropic substance abusers in different districts. Presently, there are 10 to 12 professional workers in each centre, including 0.5 to one supervisor, one centre-in-charge, and eight to ten frontline social workers. Some centres have mobilised additional resources to employ specialists, such as clinical psychologists, to enhance their competency in conducting assessment and psychotherapies. As far as effective management and operation are concerned, some centres have reorganised their services into small teams. For instance, the counselling team was formed to provide individual and group counselling, while the school team was formed to deliver preventive education programmes in schools. Some centres have also set up small teams to work in different communities within their service boundaries.

An Existential Framework for Understanding and Helping Young Substance Abusers

There have been numerous discussions, and even heated debates, about the causes and treatments of substance abuse among young people. The disease model was probably the dominant theoretical framework in the past (Brower *et al.*, 1989; Yip, 2003). Youth substance abuse was viewed as deviant and pathological, reflecting a form of maladaptive functioning due to some deficits within the individuals. It has been criticised due to its focus on young drug abusers' personal problems, which may induce society to blame them as troublemakers (McNeece and DiNitto, 2005; Norman *et al.*, 1997). The use of a cognitive model to analyse the problem of drug addiction has also become popular in recent years. The cognitive model focuses on personal mistaken attitudes, faulty beliefs, and underdeveloped analytical abilities (Igra and Irwin, 1996; Millstein and Igra, 1995). This model proposes that young people have not learned about real dangers, and thus, by supplying adequate information and guidance, they are expected to make appropriate choices. However, this framework neglects to consider a young person as a whole being encountering the existential conditions of life. For them, subjective experiences in substance abuse are their only way to get rid of life's frustrations and unpleasant feelings, thus these experiences are purposeful and meaningful (Drew, 1990).

A theoretical framework based on an existential point of view is shared and proposed here, so as to understand and draw implications for intervention and prevention for young substance abusers (Chan, 2008; To *et al.*, 2007). An existential position views youths' addictive behaviours as a manifestation of the way young people confront the stresses and challenges arising from fundamental concerns that are a part of their existence, even though this may hinder them from fostering their personal growth (Fitzgerald, 2005; Hacker, 1994; Yalom, 1982). In other words, young people experience anxiety when they fail to meet their existential needs. These repeated failing experiences accumulate and contribute to the building up of a failing identity, thus generating feelings of isolation and loss of life purpose. A young person who fails to search for existential qualities may choose to become addicted to drugs (Drew, 1990).

An existential school of psychology emerged in the sixties. The contributions of Binswanger (1958), Frankl (1964), May (1983), and Yalom (1982) are representative of this movement that focuses on helping people to discover and make sense of their own existence. An existential view of human development suggests that youths have to meet some basic needs (Bilsker, 1992; Ellsworth, 1999; Fitzgerald, 2005; Fry, 1998; Hacker, 1994), and they may turn to drugs in order to relieve anxiety in the face of these needs, namely, the struggle with identity confusion (Taubman-Ben-Ari, 2004), striving for connectedness with other people (Smith-Pickard, 2004), searching for the meaning of life (Wolf and Olenick-Shemesh, 1995), exercising freedom and responsibility (Drew, 1990), and spiritual engagement (Kruk, 2006). The proposed theoretical framework to understand the influences of these life struggles on the problem of youth drug abuse is as follows (Figure 6.1).

This framework offers a particular way of understanding the stresses that emerge in youths' confrontation with existential concerns and the possible outcomes of drug misuse. An existential view of adolescent development conceives that young people are actively engaged in identity exploration at this stage of life. Using drugs seems to be a way to relieve the emotional stresses that temporarily accompany self-doubt and role confusion (Jaynes and

Figure 6.1: Theoretical Framework

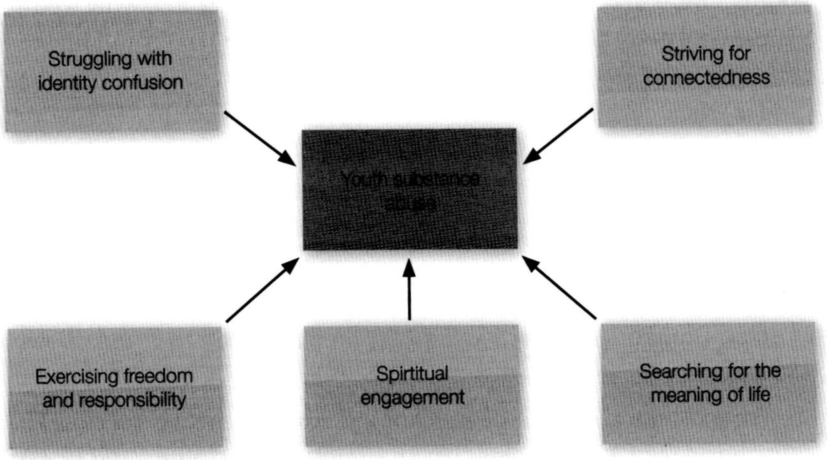

Rugg, 1988; Taubman-Ben-Ari, 2004). In addition to struggling with personal identity, the existentialists emphasise that human beings are interrelated with the world and that the world is meaningful to them (Binswanger, 1958). Smith-Pickard (2004) also regards drug addiction as a response to being in the world with others and as a way of striving for human connectedness. While young people are interested in going outside of themselves to relate to other human beings, their inability to establish an intimate relationship may lead to feelings of loneliness, social emptiness, and isolation. Drug use with peers indeed provides a sense of belonging through common values and attitudes (Baumrind and Moselle, 1985).

Existentialists also contend that people should make sense of their life experiences and foster new meanings of life. This existential concern is common during adolescence, and young people will have questions such as: what is worthwhile in my life? (Fry, 1998). Frankl (1964) holds that young people suffer from an existential vacuum, namely meaninglessness in life, which leads to emptiness and hollowness. The study of Wolf and Olenick-Shemesh (1995) also points out that losing life purpose is a contributory factor in adolescent drug addiction. Moreover, in an existential sense, we have freedom to choose our actions, yet we are responsible for our actions as well as our failures to act. Adolescence is a transitional period in learning to exercise freedom, and at the same time to face the responsibility of choosing a variety of adaptive or maladaptive behaviours to relieve the stresses arising from the existential crisis (Drew, 1990).

It is believed that spirituality is an integral dimension of the worldview and meaning systems that people use to interpret their life experience and make sense of humankind's ultimate nature (Clark, 2006). Recent research indicates that young people suffering from drug dependence experience trauma at the deepest level of their beings (Chan, 2008). Kruk (2006) also argues that when one's life is damaged by some privation, deep wounding may appear which goes beyond physical harm, psychological torment, and social exclusion. That is why young people with substance abuse often relapse after their abstinence and detoxification. Therefore, a prolonged caring and supportive environment is crucial for their spiritual engagement.

Experiences in Adopting an Existential Approach to Intervention and Prevention

We will now recount our frontline experiences of using the existential approach in working with young substance abusers. We hope that our experiences can provide some useful information for other youth workers, especially those who provide service in this field, to apply the existential approach in daily practice.

Treatment and Rehabilitation

Setting Goals of Treatment and Rehabilitation

The existential approach contends that the major causes of youth substance abuse are lack of personal identity, intimate relationships, life purposes, and spiritual engagement. It follows that interventions emphasising these aspects will be more effective than the ones focusing on the avoidance of substance abuse alone (To *et al.*, 2007). The primary goal of intervention is for young drug users to become aware of their existence as fully as possible, which includes taking charge of their lives, choosing for themselves the values and purposes that will define and guide their existence, becoming aware of their potential, and the ability to act on the basis of them (Bugental, 1978; Corey, 2001). This framework does not set out to help young people with substance abuse in the tradition of the disease model and the cognitive model. While the problem of addiction is confronted, the principal task is to explore their life's possibilities and boundaries, assist them in building a new self, and mobilise community resources in resolving their problems (van Deurzen, 2002).

Building a Therapeutic Worker-client Relationship

The first step of intervention is to establish a therapeutic relationship in which service users can experience the social worker as someone who can empathetically understand their struggles and support their efforts to reflect on their way of being (Yalom, 1982). Some practitioners may suppose that they know more about the harmful effects of substance abuse and think that young people do not know what their best interests are. They may adopt an expert's position rather than approaching the adolescents from their internal perspectives. Practitioners should view their encounter with young drug users as valuable opportunities for them to participate in their life struggles (May, 1983). By showing their understanding of how young drug users construe their life situations, practitioners can facilitate new choices.

Holistic Understanding of Clients' Needs, Strengths and Existential Sources

To develop a holistic understanding of young substance abusers' needs and strengths, all life dimensions and their relationships should be assessed comprehensively and accurately. However, practitioners are accustomed to focusing on the symptoms, deficits, and problems encountered by clients rather than their needs, strengths, and feelings. Moreover, analysing the existential sources of substance abuse, especially the spiritual dimension, is still a neglected arena in frontline practice (Chan, 2004). Drug addicts accumulate intense feelings of alienation, separateness, emptiness, and meaninglessness. They use drugs to enhance their sense of self-control, power, aggressiveness, and sexual competence, for which they have been deprived for years (Langer and Beneveneto, 1978; Peele, 1985). Social workers should understand that the feelings of taking drugs are embedded in clients' inner experience and are good and attractive (Yip, 2003). The abusers may try to intensify these feelings by increasing the dosage of drugs. It also provides a good explanation of why drug addicts go back to the old way of being soon after detoxification. In other words, practitioners do not find themselves in a linear helping process, but rather move back and forth among different phases of treatment and rehabilitation.

Assisting Clients in Manifesting an Authentic Existence

Creating a constructive climate for young drug takers to analyse their needs, strengths and existential sources of substance abuse is crucial. Having recognised that the old way of being is not working, the social worker can facilitate the seeking of alternatives to deal with their life concerns and help addicts recognise their competence to make personal transformations (Bugental, 1978). Practitioners should help clients look beyond their fears and limitations and discover something inspirational and meaningful (Sermabeikian, 1994). They have to facilitate clients' examination of the implications of their decisions for the purposes and values they are choosing to guide their existence (Corey, 2001). In addition to individual counselling, practitioners can achieve these goals through running mutual support groups (Chan, 2008). Through the groups, participants can listen to other members' stories, vent their negative emotions, widen their perspectives of themselves and the world around them, learn better ways to communicate with and support each other, and reaffirm their strengths. Furthermore, helping clients search for the meaning of life is not enough. Practitioners have to encourage clients to implement their chosen life purposes in daily practice. It is difficult in the sense that drug abusers have accumulated thoughts and response habits over a period of time, and these habits may continue to influence their feelings and behaviour, even though they want to relate to themselves and the world in a new way. They should be instilled with hope and appreciated for their efforts in striving to take charge of their lives, and encouraged not to give up (van Deurzen, 2002). In brief, clients' motivation and involvement in treatment and rehabilitation are based on positive feelings such as being respected, understood, cared for, and appreciated in the process.

Mobilising Social Support in Helping Clients Reintegrate into the Community

Building social support and networks is a crucial factor in the course of treatment and rehabilitation for young substance abusers. Once clients abandon their using habits, a caring and healthy social environment could help them keep away from undesirable influences. In the past few years, one of the authors organised a mutual support group for substance abusers based on a spiritual perspective (Chan, 2008). He mobilised community resources such as churches' support for young drug abusers' spiritual engagement. Unlike social services that might cease after the termination of cases and groups, concerned churches were able to provide continuous pastoral care to ex-substance abusers. Having constructive adult role models who came from churches expanded youths' life experiences, helped them build up close relationships, fostered an improved personal identity, and redirected them from risk-taking behaviours. They also invited these young ex-drug abusers to join church activities, which facilitated their continuous recovery and reintegration into the community.

Prevention

Drug prevention is a top priority in Hong Kong, and lots of resources are devoted to preventive education and publicity. Existing drug prevention programmes often consist of two components, namely enhancing adolescents' awareness of the adverse effects of illicit drugs and educating them to "say no to drugs" (McNeece and DiNitto, 2005). Such components are closely aligned with the disease model and cognitive model. Although these models shed some light into the understanding of youth substance abuse, accumulated research findings indicate the inadequacy of the related programmes (Norman *et al.*, 1997). Johnston (1990) suggests that equipping young people with information and knowledge about drugs, in conjunction with other preventive approaches, is the most effective strategy.

Enhancing Young People's Knowledge about Substance Abuse

In Hong Kong, knowledge-based drug prevention programmes, which involve enhancing young people's knowledge of drug effects, recent trends and modes of drug taking, peer influences, anti-drug laws and law enforcement, are delivered to students to raise their awareness of substance misuse. In order to impress the participants, former substance abusers would be invited to share their experience and take the initiative to chat with participants. For those students who have taken drugs occasionally, former abusers could encourage them to be alert to any health problems caused by substance abuse and motivate them to seek early treatment.

Organising Multifaceted Drug Prevention Programmes

Multifaceted programmes for drug prevention should be designed for young people. Practitioners can collaborate with school personnel and other welfare organisations to conduct life enrichment programmes. These programmes can promote constructive psychological development of young people through cultivating a positive self-image and a sense of belonging. They can contribute to the cognitive development of young people through a critical assessment of life issues and an application of knowledge to respond to these issues. Moreover, they can create chances for young people to take part in volunteer services and community programmes so that they can rethink their lifestyles, rights and responsibilities, and roles in society (To, 2007). All these aspects can assist adolescents in dealing with existential conflicts and learning to become autonomous and self-actualized (Taubman-Ben-Ari, 2004).

Synthesising the Existential Approach and Other Youth Work Approaches

There is a growing trend towards the synthesis of different youth work approaches. In recent years some intellectuals have suggested strengthening the protective factors in schools that can foster resiliency in young people (Kaplan, 1999). Some initiated a multifaceted collaborative effort to enlist school and community members in making the surrounding social systems more conducive to competence, character, connection, confidence, and contribution building (Pittman *et al.*, 2001). These approaches are in many ways parallel to an existential framework. They challenge the deficit model of youth work and offer practical approaches in creating a facilitative environment that prevents young people from succumbing to substance abuse. Families, schools, and social organisations play important roles in helping young drug users to deal with existential crises. The resilient approach and positive youth development approach also emphasise collaborative efforts among the government, community members, social workers, educators, and parents in enhancing young people's adaptive potential in stressful life events. As such, we can synthesise the existential framework and other youth work approaches for drug prevention.

Conclusion

Youth substance abuse is one of the pervasive social problems in Hong Kong. It can lead to damaging effects on young people, their families, schools, communities, and society at large. An existential perspective is adopted to theorise a conceptual framework to aid in understanding and working with young drug takers. The authors' field experiences also indicate the effectiveness and full spectrum of adopting an existential approach to intervention and prevention. If drug taking is instrumental in reducing a sense of emptiness, gaining care and concern from significant others, and discovering "who they are" and "where they go," the existing policies and services for tackling youth substance abuse should be thoroughly revisited.

References

Baumrind, D. and Moselle, K. A. (1985). "A Developmental Perspective on Adolescent Drug Abuse," In *Alcohol and Substance Abuse in Adolescence*, edited by B. Stimmel, pp. 41–68. New York: The Haworth Press.

Bilsker, D. (1992). "An Existentialist Account of Identity Formation," *Journal of Adolescence, Volume 15*, pp. 177–192.

Binswanger, L. (1958). "The Existential Analysis School of Thought," In *Existence: A New Dimension in Psychiatry and Psychology*, edited by R. May, E. Angel and H. F. Ellenberger, pp. 191–213. New York: Basic Books.

Brower, K. J., Blow, F. C. and Beresford, T. P. (1989). "Treatment Implications of Chemical Dependency Models: An Integrated Approach," *Journal of Substance Abuse Treatment, Volume 6*, pp. 147–157.

Bugental, J. F. T. (1978). *Psychotherapy and Process: The Fundamentals of an Existential-Humanistic Approach.* New York: Random House.

Chan, K. K. (2004). *A Spiritual Group for the Drug Addicts.* (Unpublished master's practice based project). Hong Kong: Hong Kong Polytechnic University.

Chan, K. K. (2008). "Spiritual Support Group for Persons with Substance Abuse: A Strengths Perspective," In *Strength Based Perspective in Working with Clients with Mental Illness: A Chinese Cultural Articulation*, edited by K. S. Yip, pp. 298–300. New York: Nova Science Publishers.

Chan, K. K. and Chung Y. H. (in press). "Substance Abuse and Treatment Mode in Hong Kong: From One Dimension to Multi-dimensions," In *Handbook on Youth Mental Health*, edited by Hong Kong Council of Social Service. Hong Kong: Hong Kong Council of Social Service. (in Chinese)

Cheung, Y. W. and Cheung, W. T. (2006). "Is Hong Kong Experiencing Normalization of Adolescent Drug Use? Some Reflections on the Normalization Thesis," *Substance Use and Misuse, Volume 41*, pp. 1967–1990.

Clark, J. L. (2006). "Listening for Meaning: A Research-based Model for Attending to Spirituality, Culture and Worldview in Social Work Practice," *Critical Social Work, Volume 7 (1).* Retrieved 10 June 2008, from www.criticalsocialwork.com/units/socialwork/critical.nsf/inToc/29CBE19CA5952C3985257179006FF85B

Corey, G. (2001). *Theory and Practice of Counseling and Psychotherapy.* Stamford, Conn.: Brooks/Cole.

Drew, L. R. H. (1990). "Facts We Don't Want to Face," *Drug and Alcohol Review, Volume 9*, pp. 207–210.

Ellsworth, J. (1999). "Today's Adolescent: Addressing Existential Dread," *Adolescence, Volume 34 (134)*, pp. 403–408.

Fitzgerald, B. (2005). "An Existential View of Adolescent Development," *Adolescence, Volume 40 (160)*, pp. 795–799.

Frankl, V. E. (1964). *Man's Search for Meaning: An Introduction to Logotherapy.* London: Hodder and Stoughton.

Fry, P. S. (1998). "The Development of Personal Meaning and Wisdom in Adolescence: A Reexamination of Moderating and Consolidating Factors and Influences," In *The Human Quest for Meaning: A Handbook of Psychological Research and Clinical Applications*, edited by T. P. Wong and P. S. Fry Mahwah, pp. 91–110. N.J.: Lawrence Erlbaum Associates.

Hacker, D. J. (1994). "An Existential View of Adolescence," *Journal of Early Adolescence, Volume 14 (3)*, pp. 300–327.

Igra, V. and Irwin, C. E., Jr. (1996). "Theories of Adolescent Risk-taking Behavior," In *Ponton Handbook of Adolescent Health Risk Behavior*, edited by R. J. Diclemente, W. B. Hansen and L. E., pp. 35–51. New York: Plenum Press.

Irwin, C. E., Jr. (1993). "Adolescence and Risk Taking: How Are They Related?" In *Adolescent Risk Taking*, edited by N. J. Bell and R. W. Bell, pp. 7–28. Newbury Park: Sage.

Jaynes, J. H. and Rugg, C. A. (1988). *Adolescents, Alcohol and Drugs: A Practical Guide for Those who Work with Young People*. Illinois: Charles C. Thomas Publisher.

Johnston, L. D. (1990). *Reducing Drug Use in America: A Perspective, A Strategy, and Some Promising Approaches*. Michigan: The University of Michigan Institute for Social Research.

Kaplan, H. B. (1999). "Toward an Understanding of Resilience: A Critical Review of Definitions and Models," In *Resilience and Development: Positive Life Adaptations*, edited by M. D. Glantz and J. H. Johnson, pp. 17–83. New York: Kluwer Academic/Plenum.

Kruk, E. (2006). "Spiritual Wounding and Affliction: Facilitating Spiritual Transformation in Social Justice Work," *Critical Social Work, Volume 7 (1)*. Retrieved 10 June 2008, from www.criticalsocialwork.com/units/socialwork/critical.nsf/inToc/29CBE19CA5952C398525717900 6FF85B.

Lam, C. W., Weng, B. W., Wong, O. O. and Tse, S. K. (2004). *A Study of Substance Abuse in Underground Rave Culture and other Related Settings*. Hong Kong: Narcotic Division.

Langer, E. J. and Benventon, A. (1978). "Self-induced Dependence," *Journal of Personality and Social Psychology, Volume 36*, pp. 886–893.

Lau, T. F. (2003). *Research Report on Cross-Boundary Substance Abuse Problem among Youths in Hong Kong*. Hong Kong: Narcotics Division.

May, R. (1983). *The Discovery of Being: Writings in Existential Psychology*. New York: W. W. Norton.

McNeece, C. A. and DiNitto, D. M. (2005). *Chemical Dependency: A Systems Approach*. Boston: Pearson.

Millstein, S. G. and Igra, V. (1995). "Theoretical Models of Adolescent Risk-taking Behavior," In *Adolescent Health Problems: Behavioral Perspectives*, edited by J. L. Wallander and L. J. Siegel, pp. 52–71. New York: Guilford Press.

Narcotics Division (2003). *Central Registry of Drug Abuse: Forty-seven Report (1984–2003)*. Hong Kong: Hong Kong SAR Government.

Narcotics Division (2006). *Central Registry of Drug Abuse: Fifty-six Report (1997–2006)*. Hong Kong: Hong Kong SAR Government.

Narcotics Division (2007). *Hong Kong Narcotics and Anti-money Laundering Report 2006*. Hong Kong Hong Kong SAR Government.

Narcotics Division (2008). *News Release: Anti-drug Measures of Task Force on Youth Drug Abuse*. Retrieved 10 June 2008 from www.info.gov.hk/gia/general/200806/04/P200806040204.htm.

Ngai, S. S. Y., Ngai, N. P. and Cheung, C. K. (2006). *Risk-taking Behavior among Hong Kong Young Dance Partygoers: What They Do and Why?* Hong Kong: Department of Social Work, the Chinese University of Hong Kong.

Norman, E., Turner, S., Zunz, S. J. and Stillson, K. (1997). "Prevention Programs Reviewed: What Works?" In *Drug-free Youth: A Compendium for Prevention Specialists*, edited by E. Norman, pp. 22–45. New York: Garland Publishing.

Peele, S. (1985). *The Meaning of Addiction*. Toronto: Lexington Press.

Pittman, K., Irby, M. and Ferber, T. (2001). "Unfinished Business: Further Reflections on a Decade of Promoting Youth Development," In *Trends in Youth Development: Visions, Realities and Challenges*, edited by P. L. Benson and K. J. Pittman, pp. 3–50. Boston: Kluwer Academic Publishers.

Sermabeikian, P. (1994). "Our Clients, Ourselves: The Spiritual Perspective and Social Work Practice," *Social Work, Volume 39 (2)*, pp. 178–183.

Smith-Pickard, P. (2004). "The Locus of Addiction," *Existential Analysis, Volume 15 (1)*, pp. 55–72.

Taubman-Ben-Ari, O. (2004). "Risk Taking in Adolescence: 'To Be or Not To Be' is Not Really the Question," In *Handbook of Experimental*

Existential Psychology, edited by J. Greenberg, S. L. Koole and T. Psyzczynski, pp. 104–121. New York: Guilford Press.

To, S. M. (2007). "Empowering School Social Work Practices for Positive Youth Development: Hong Kong Experience," *Adolescence, Volume 42*, pp. 555–567.

To, S. M., Ngai, S. S. Y., Ngai, N. P. and Cheung, C. K. (2007). "Young People's Existential Concerns and Club Drug Abuse," *International Journal of Adolescence and Youth, Volume 13*, pp. 327–341.

Wolf, Y. and Olenick-Shemesh, D. (1995). "Personal and Situational Factors in Drug Use as Perceived by Kibbutz Youth," *Adolescence, Volume 30 (120)*, pp. 909–931.

van Deurzen, E. (2002). *Existential Counseling and Psychotherapy in Practice*. London: Sage.

Yalom, I. D. (1982). *Existential Psychotherapy*. New York: Basic Books.

Yip, K. S. (2003). "A Strengths Perspective in Working with an Adolescent with Dual Diagnosis," *Clinical Social Work Journal, Volume 31 (2)*, pp. 189–203.

7

WORKING WITH YOUTH-AT-RISK THROUGH ADVENTURE COUNSELLING PROGRAMMES: THE CASE OF FEMALE SUBSTANCE ABUSERS

*Alex Tak-shing LEE, Kennedy Kwok-hung NG, Wun-tsz HO,
Fanny King-har WONG, Daisy Ming-lai LO*

Introduction

With the rising number of young female substance abusers in the past years, more and more organisations have targeted their services to serving these girls with different approaches. In only the first half of 2006, the number of female substance abusers rose by 1.6% and stood at 2,158 (Narcotics Division, 2006).

This chapter aims to explore the possibility of working with the young female substance abusers in a residential treatment setting through the holistic approach of adventure counselling programme.

Young Substance Abusers in Hong Kong

Drug abuse refers to the taking of drugs without following medical advice or prescription, or the indiscreet use of dangerous drugs for non-treatment purposes. Here we use the term substance abuse to represent the situation. Based on the statistics from the Central Registry of Drug Abuse (CRDA) of the Narcotics Division of the Government, the total number of substance abusers in the first half of 2006 was 7,941, 11.5% lower than that of the same period in 2005 which was 8,969 (Narcotics Division, 2006). However, the number of female substance abusers and the number of young substance abusers aged under 21 were alarming. For those aged under 21, the number rose by 10.4%. According to the information released on 24 January 2007 from CRDA, in the first three-quarters of 2006, the most commonly abused substance by young substance abusers is Ketamine, followed by Ecstasy and Cannabis.

The number of poly-substance abusers was also on the rise. The proportion of youngsters under 21 taking multiple substances was much higher, and was at 53.8% of the total reported cases. Taking multiple substances is more popular among the psychotropic substance abusers (70.5%) (Narcotics Division, 2006). There are a lot of factors that influenced them to take multiple substances, such as identification with peers, relief of boredom and seeking euphoria, as well as the misconception of harmless effects of psychotropic substances. As stated in the CRDA report (Narcotics Division, 2006), the reasons for young substance abusers taking drugs could be summarised as follows: (1) identifying with peers (46.1%), (2) avoiding the discomfort of withdrawal (42.5%), and (3) relieving boredom/depression/anxiety (32.8%).

Substance Abuse Treatment and Rehabilitation Services in Hong Kong

In the provision of treatment and rehabilitation services, Hong Kong adopts a multi-modality approach for drug dependent persons of different backgrounds. Services can be grouped into the following five categories: (1) compulsory placement scheme operated by the Correctional Services Department (CSD); (2) voluntary out-patient methadone treatment program provided by the Department of Health (DH); (3) voluntary in-patient programmes run by the Caritas-Hong Kong, the Society for the Aid and Rehabilitation of Drug Abusers (SARDA), the Hong Kong Christian Service (HKCS), and other non-governmental organisations (NGOs) (e.g. some Christian agencies); (4) counselling services for psychotropic substance abusers provided by the Caritas—HUGS Centre, PS33 of the HKCS, Cheer Lutheran Centre and Evergreen Lutheran Centre of Hong Kong Lutheran Social Service (HKLSS) and Tung Wah Group of Hospitals CROSS Centre; and (5) substance abuse clinics operated by the Hospital Authority (HA) (Narcotics Division, 2007).

In recent years, some organisations are providing treatment and rehabilitation services especially for female substance abusers. For young female substance abusers, providing new experiences for them to learn, to grow and to change can be very significant to their lives. It is believed that employing an adventure counselling approach in working with young female substance abusers can provide them with experiences as avenues for the development of positive characters. It can also help them to experience feelings in greater depth, and hopefully feel better about themselves, others and the world that they live in.

The following story reveals what a typical young female substance abuser looks like and her responses towards the experiential-based training using an adventure counselling approach in the treatment process.

Story of Mary (make-up names are used for confidentiality)

Mary had started to take psychotropic substances when she was 16. She said that after taking the substances, she could release the unbearable feelings of helplessness and restlessness arising from her work, family and unhappy emotional life. Her abuse of substances was subsequently discovered by family members. After discovery by her family and being persuaded by her family repeatedly, she voluntarily joined the one-year residential detoxification treatment programme of an NGO at age 20. The treatment process was divided into two phases, and took place in the training centre and halfway centre of the agency, respectively. In the training centre, an adventure counselling programme was carried out in the afternoons of Wednesdays, Thursdays and Fridays. At that time, her weight was 96 pounds, and she had just got over physical dependence on the substances. With her weak physique, her jogging was slow, her feet were feeble, and her pulse accelerated easily. She tired easily and wanted to give up. With the encouragement of the other girls, she finally managed to finish the training.

After a period of time, she finished different stages of the training with a sense of success and self-confidence, and then began to think of a higher goal. In the past, she used to think of herself as incapable of achieving anything, but then, she learned how to break down a seemingly impossible large goal into small tasks. By finishing the small tasks one by one, she would then achieve her ultimate goal. Furthermore, in an encouraging environment, she no longer experienced loneliness, but rather, warmth and support.

While Mary still needed to face a variety of difficulties in life, she had found a new way of coping. Instead of giving up automatically, she had learned how to endure patiently, solve questions bit by bit, and seek support in her surroundings. The fact that she could face the challenge calmly with others was precisely the accumulated outcome of the continuous experiential-based training. Mary could then move on and was ready to take on bigger challenges. That is exactly the expected effect of an adventure counselling programme. Now, let us introduce the basic concepts of adventure counselling.

Historical Background of Development of Adventure Counselling (AC)

In 1941, Dr. Kurt Hahn initiated the systemic development of adventure education by establishing the Wales Outward Bound movement. In 1958, the first Outward Bound School was established by Hahn for youth (Priest and Gass, 1997). In 1970, Jerry Pieh brought the original roots of the Outward Bound movement back to the school setting in the form of curriculum for youth development. He established the organisation "Project Adventure Inc." for working with young people in school settings by using the methodology of "Adventure-Based Counselling" (ABC) (Prouty, 1990).

The development of the AC in Hong Kong is based on the conceptual framework and methodology of ABC (Adventure-Based Counselling) with local adaptations and concerns. The authors use the term "adventure counselling" instead of "adventure-based counselling" owing to the registration system conducted by Project Adventure Inc. (Lee and Mak, 2002). In Hong Kong, AC is employed as the major intervention in children and youth programmes, especially in Understanding the Adolescent Project (UAP)—a programme subsidized by the Social Welfare Department and Education and Manpower Bureau for building resilience among youth-at-risk in secondary and primary schools (Choi *et al.*, 2003).

Definition and Main Goal of AC

It is not easy to define AC since the conceptual framework and the then methods used are so broad. As Schoel, Prouty and Radcliffe (1988:11–12) stated that there is the "openness" of ABC for educators, counsellors, therapists or other professionals to make use of the ABC activities, and they are encouraged to "define their own theoretical rationale" and re-define the respective "theoretical assumptions" frequently with professional community sharing.

According to Lee and Mak (2002:24–8), adventures could be defined as "doing something new." When the participants do something new, they are requested to move out of their personal psychological "comfort zone." Participants are faced with challenges and tackle "edge experience," which provides the "teachable moment" for the participants to acknowledge their competence and self-concept. This process provides opportunities for personal growth of the participants. Thus, AC could be described as a model of counselling by making use of a series of well designed adventure programming, therapeutically aiming at participants' personal growth. In Hong Kong, AC is a kind of counselling tool for improving the self-concept of participants (Choi *et al.*, 2003).

With reference to Lee and Mak (2002), adventure interventions include (1) adventure recreation or tour, (2) adventure training, (3) adventure education, (4) adventure counselling, and (5) adventure therapy. By identifying the goals, counselling elements employed, and intensity level of the intervention applied by the different adventure programmes, they can be classified into these five categories. Making use of adventures or wilderness activities or adventure training are not the same as AC. Some workers input the elements from TV shows such as Survivor, Boot Camp or Military Camp to the AC programmes. These programmes may have adventure or wilderness elements but they could not be classified as adventure counselling or therapy since there are no counselling or therapeutic elements in the programmes (Itin, 2001).

The authors recommend the definition of AC as proposed by Itin (2001:81) as making use of "adventure-base practice" to effect a positive change in "behavior, affect and/or cognition." This definition indicates the importance of clinical theoretical framework (conceptualisation), processing elements (required counselling techniques and skills for debriefing), and expected outcomes (the way to go) of the AC programme for clients in order to facilitate them in creating effective changes in behaviour, emotion, and cognition (Russell, 2001).

Theoretical Framework of AC for Hong Kong Practice

According to Fletcher and Hinkle (2002), AC theory was developed from various counselling theories such as Beck's cognitive, Ellis's emotive behavioural, Glasser's reality, Bandura and Skinner's behavioural, Zinker's Gestalt, Bruner's Narrative, and Fosnot's Constructivist theories. The authors agree that cognitive theory is the major theoretical framework for AC practice since it deals with clients holistically including cognitive, behavioural, emotional, and underlying psychological mechanisms (Persons, 1989). Lee and Mak (2002) recognize the elements of the AC theoretical framework, namely, (1) dynamic counselling, (2) adventure, (3) wilderness, (4) experiential learning, and (5) workers' use of self. This framework will be further explained.

Elements for Practising AC

AC cannot be separated from the therapeutic use of adventure key elements, activities, and programming elements. The key elements of AC include (1) Trust Building, (2) Goal Setting, (3) Challenge/Stress, (4) Humour/Fun/Joy/Celebration, (5) Peak Experience, and (6) Problem-solving (Schoel *et al.*, 1988). Lee and Mak (2002) recognise a seventh element, namely, (7) Social Responsibility. All these key elements exist in all successful AC programmes. They work together like a "matrix of seven pillars" and not in a linear or sequential order for facilitating improvement of participants' self-concept (Prouty, 1990).

The activities of AC consist of (1) Ice Breaker/Acquaintance (e.g. Name Game), (2) De-Inhibitizer (e.g. Funny Face), (3) Trust and Empathy (e.g. Willow-in-the-wind), (4) Communication (e.g. Blindfold Polygon), (5) Decision-making/Problem-solving (e.g. Spider's Web), (6) Social Responsibility (e.g. Service Learning), and (7) Personal Responsibility (e.g. Challenge Course). All these activities are organised into an adventure wave plan with good sequencing for facilitating clients' improvement of self-concept (Schoel *et al.*, 1988).

According to Fletcher and Hinkle (2002), AC programming elements include: (1) Setting for promoting therapeutic use of environment, process, place, and relationship, (2) Programming skills for assessment, appropriate conditions for learning, sequencing of the activities, and debriefing, (3) Intensity of perceived risk level for arousing clients' holistic functioning, including behavioural, cognitive and emotional in respect to change, (4) Counselling skills, including soft skills, hard skills, meta skills (integrating ability in hard and soft skills), generic competence, and specific competence for facilitating clients motivation, (5) Clients' disequilibrium, (6) Marco-processing for debriefing, and (7) Transferring adventure experience and benefit to real life application.

Practical Wisdoms of Working in AC

The authors have identified, from frontline experience, that dynamic counselling, therapeutic adventure and wilderness elements, experiential learning, AC counsellors' use of self, and therapeutic use of spirituality are important elements in working with substance abuse relapse prevention.

Casework Framework: Cognitive Therapy (CT) as a Tool for Case Formulation

Cheung, Lee and Lee (2003) consider that the Cognitive-Behavioural Approach (CBA) is the most effective treatment for substance abuse rehabilitation services in Hong Kong. It unlocks the important issue of substance abuse: long-term relapse prevention through "favourable cognitive development and appropriate behavioral skills" (Cheung *et al.*, 2003:195). Cheung *et al.* (2003) have shown that CBA can apply techniques used for Ellis's Rational-Emotive Therapy and Beck's Cognitive Therapy.

According to Persons (1989), psychological problems occur at two levels, namely, overt difficulties and underlying psychological mechanism. The underlying psychological mechanism refers to one or multiple irrational or distorted beliefs about the self of the individual. The overt difficulties are again classified into two levels, namely macro and micro levels. The micro level of overt difficulties is when the problems can be expressed in terms of three components: cognitions, behaviours, and moods. There are two relationships among the components, namely synchrony and interdependence. A synchrony relationship means that problems found in one component are also present in other components at the same time. An interdependence relationship means that a change in any one component is likely to produce changes in the other components. In view of this, intervention could take place for any components in order to change the whole system. The relationship between overt difficulties and underlying mechanisms is in the form of bi-directional arrows. Changes at one level could create changes at other level.

According to Beck *et al.* (1993:22–7), the process of substance abuse creates a vicious cycle, since abusers need to get a greater amount of the substance to maintain the same level of arousal or to eradicate negative emotions owing to withdrawal side effects. Worse still, this process establishes the abusers' sense of helplessness in controlling their craving. Thus, the main aim of CT treatment is to reduce clients' destructive emotional reactions, self-defeating behaviours, and maladaptive beliefs or thinking through the treatment. Beck constructs a Complete Model of Substance Use which is a sequence of situations and beliefs including Activating Stimulus (internal and external), Activation of Beliefs, Automatic Thoughts, Craving/Urges, Facilitating Beliefs, Focus on Instrumental Strategies, and Relapse. Beck points out that the therapeutic tasks for substance abuse are conceptual change and technical development of proficiency in coping. With reference to Person's Case Formulation Approach and Beck's CT on Substance Abuse, more insights for working with female substance abusers through AC are obtained.

According to Person's Case Formulation Approach, clients' conceptual change could be facilitated from any components of behavioural, cognitive, emotional, or underlying psychological mechanisms, since their relationships are synchrony, interdependence, and bi-directionalness. AC elements such as hiking, backpacking, and wild camping are ideal tools for facilitating the changes in clients (Caulkins *et al.*, 2006). The facilitation usually starts with the behavioural component, since AC programming in the wilderness or adventure requires clients to perform physical exercises. Clients experience changes in behavioural components such as improvement of physical fitness, competence, and endurance. The clients' change in behavioural components leads to cognitive changes, such as the clients' sense of competence (e.g. I am in control! I am not helpless!), sense of belongingness (e.g. I am loved!), and sense of optimism (e.g. I believe there will be a way in my life!). These behavioural and cognitive changes lead to the improvement in emotional and underlying psychological mechanisms. This process helps break the vicious cycle and sense of helplessness of clients in substance abuse and facilitates their motivation for change. Improvement of these three components reduces the risk of relapse owing to the activation of beliefs, automatic thoughts, and facilitating beliefs. All these beliefs originate from the underlying psychological mechanisms due to the unmet need of clients in their self-concepts of competence, belonging, and optimism (Beck *et al.*, 1993).

Group Work: Yalom's Process Group Approach

Weiss *et al.* (2004) define group therapy as the group process of participants where the interaction among them is regarded as the basic therapeutic factor. They recognise the primary goals of eliminating substance use are: (1) group education model, (2) recovery skills training, (3) group process model, (4) check-in-group, and (5) anger management or parenting skills.

Using Yalom's Process Group Approach (Yalom and Leszcz, 2005) in AC practice could fulfil the primary goals listed above owing to the therapeutic use of experiential learning, interpersonal learning, working in the here-and-now, facilitating group cohesiveness, and the 11 therapeutic factors (Ward and Litchy, 2004). These elements facilitate clients in dealing with their difficulties in relationships, especially in interpersonal conflict resolution (Beck *et al.*, 1993).

The group process itself is a therapeutic tool for AC substance abuse group. As Yalom and Leszcz (2005:143) define the "process" as "the nature of the relationship between interacting individuals—members and therapist." It provides a new and alternative opportunity for interpersonal learning including: (1) importance of interpersonal relationships, (2) corrective emotional experience, (3) provision of social microcosm as a dynamic interaction in group, (4) increased awareness and recognition of behavioural patterns in social microcosm, and (5) gained transference and insight in microcosm (Yalom and Leszcz, 2005). AC programming is an experiential learning and healing therapeutic group for clients in dealing with their relationship problems or conflicts within the group. This process could tackle clients' coping strategy of using substances for alleviating their stress in those relationships. The group itself is therapeutic, which facilitates clients in re-connecting with other members in a social microcosm setting to form a self-help healing community.

The 11 therapeutic factors, as listed below, can facilitate clients in creating change in an AC group: (1) Instillation of Hope: providing optimism for clients' improvement, (2) University: having similar feelings about problems as other participants, so that they are not alone or special, (3) Imparting Information: seeking advice from therapist or participants, (4) Altruism: participants gaining a positive view of self by helping others, (5) Corrective Recapitulation of Primary Family Group: re-enacting some critical familial issues in corrective ways within the group, (6) Development of Socialisation Techniques: providing an environment for interacting in adaptive and constructive ways, (7) Imitative Behaviour: providing constructive communication pattern-modelling to clients, (8) Interpersonal Learning: facilitating interpersonal learning through sharing, observation and practice, (9) Group Cohesiveness: giving a feeling of togetherness, (10) Catharsis: releasing past or here-and-now feelings in order to feel better, and (11) Existential Factors: giving the message of self-responsibility in their lives (Kivlighan and Holmes, 2004; Yalom and Leszcz, 2005).

Therapeutic Use of Adventure and Wilderness Elements

Although there is some evidence of the efficacy of using adventure or wilderness elements, there is not much clinical research on the topic. The majority of research consists of qualitative exploratory studies on the topic of adventure or wilderness (Caulkins *et al.*, 2006). The study done by Caulkins *et al.* (2006) has revealed that wilderness experience could give the participants a "sense of accomplishment, increasing their perceptions of their own competence...feeling of self-efficacy, increased awareness of oneself and others, and of one's immediate surroundings, and finally a sense of timelessness." (Caulkins *et al.*, 2006:33–4) Wilderness experiences could give clients a sense of competence, especially in awareness of personal physical fitness, perception of self-efficacy, emotional control, locus of control, and courage in tackling challenges in life. In addition, wilderness experience itself is a healing timeless moment for clients to relax and reflect on their here-and-now situation in a spiritual dimension. It provides clients with an inner space for re-connecting, reframing and creating meaning of their stories existentially and spiritually.

In the study conducted by Russell and Phillips-Miller (2002), four key findings are recognised: (1) relationship with counsellor/therapist, (2) peer dynamics, (3) facilitated reflection on life through use of "solo" activities, and (4) challenges and structure of the process (Russell and Phillips-Miller, 2002:415–37). This research helps us to understand the importance of the relationship in AC in working with female substance abusers. AC programming starts with relationship-building in a caring and supportive environment. It emphasises relationship-building among the participants themselves (intra-personal), peer and therapists (inter-personal), and creating meaning in their existence (existential and spiritual relationship). This is the first step for motivating clients to tackle life challenges.

The above indicates the importance of relationship-building (Beringer, 2004) and competence in nurturing through AC programming. These findings are very close to those we find from dynamic counselling. Dynamic counselling could be integrated in the application of adventure or wilderness elements. This application could ignite clients' improvement in terms of belongingness (interpersonal), competence (recognizing self-competence, feeling of accomplishment, emotional management, personal locus of control) and optimism (intrapersonal searching for meaning of life) for change (Choi *et al.*, 2003).

Power of Experiential Learning

Beard and Wilson (2002) pointed out that the use of adventure and wilderness elements in AC could facilitate the participants to learn more deeply and effectively. They define experiential learning as "insight gained through the conscious or unconscious internalisation of our own or observed experiences, which build upon our past experience or knowledge" (Beard and Wilson, 2002:39). AC programming could provide various opportunities for enhancing participants' capacity to learn through debriefing, owing to its nature of requiring multiple skills and facing unforeseeable variety. The enrichment of emotional experience through AC programming is the key to facilitating learning and engagement in the group.

The essence of experiential learning provided by adventure or wilderness elements is facilitating how natural emotions work on clients through a real microcosm for social connection, interpersonal communication, emotional experience in a group and a real living setting. These adventure and wilderness experiences (e.g. camping) provide real everyday living situations and facilitate clients in experiencing, being aware, reflection, being responsible in their lives, consolidation, and transferring their learning from the group to daily living.

Therapeutic Humanware of Adventure Counsellor

According to Cartwright (1987), the roles of an AC counsellor are being an expert facilitator and a psychological supporter to clients. These roles reveal the importance of the humanware of an AC counsellor. The "therapeutic use of self" of an AC counsellor is the core part of programming which provides a sense of physical safety, psychological security, care and support for facilitating as well as processing the change of clients in case and group work. It is also a precious moment for clients to "unlearn" past dysfunctional interpersonal or intra-personal patterns and to establish new functional interpersonal skills in the social microcosm created by the AC programming. This is the process in which clients become aware of and reflect on alternatives for their lives (Satir, 1987). Moreover, it brings out the therapeutic relationship with participants and makes the process itself therapeutic (Coady and Wolgein, 1996). The effectiveness of the AC programming is highly dependent on the integration of the counsellors' use of self in the perspective of personal, professional and technical aspects (Edwards and Bess, 1998). The therapists' technical use of self could be the entry and contact point for engaging with the clients, as the therapists can establish trust and empathy with clients. Coupled with this, the therapists' professional self can make use of skills training as a tool for front-loading the metaphor for framing the adventure or wilderness experiences, as well as transferring the meaning of the experience to real life. All these techniques involve professional training of the therapists in case and group work. The therapists' personal use of self is the most important asset, since it involves therapeutic use of self in the perspectives of personal experiences and personality.

Therapeutic Use of Spirituality

Although, there is a lack of systematic empirical research for validating the effectiveness and efficacy on spirituality intervention on substance abuse, especially concerning the attributes of spirituality and substance abuse behavioural change, Neff and MacMaster (2005) propose the Integrative Conceptual Model of Spiritual Mechanisms Underlying Substance Abuse Behaviour Change for exploring the underlying conceptualisation and theoretical mechanism of the issue. The Model includes four important aspects: (1) Individual Attributes, (2) Program Elements, (3) Social Learning Process, and (4) Spiritual Transformation Process leading to behavioural change. All these elements are crucial factors for working with substance-abuse clients. Individual attributes of the clients are important to the intervention since they indicate clients' "initial levels of spirituality" and "initial treatment readiness" for the intervention. Clients' individual attributes include their willingness and motivation for change. The elements of "Faith Based Intervention" in the programme include empathy, acceptance, forgiveness, discipline, norms, and support. These elements provide clients with a meaning and ideology of life in terms of spiritual interpretation. All these elements are reinforced by the social learning processes in terms of mentors' role-modelling and social reinforcement within the spiritual community. The spiritual transformation processes involve the "identification of the self with the scared" by inducing a new meaning in life. This is a shifting process of self-forgiveness from "negative to positive coping strategies" (Neff and MacMaster, 2005:671–5).

With reference to Ng (1999), "religious beliefs" serve as a "cognitive mediator" for creating meaning for clients in understanding and interpreting their lives. Moreover, it provides the opportunity for the "process of re-socialization into Christian identity" and re-connects them with themselves with "total acceptance" (Ng, 1999:559).

Disequilibrium and Risk Application in AC

Rock climbing and abseiling are high events that have been employed in the AC programme for the female substance abusers. There were lots of questions for practicing these high events. What was the main aim of these high event programmes? Were we applying disequilibrium or risk for facilitating clients to change? Were the participants ready for these high events? Were these challenges or disequilibrium promoting clients' growth? Were these risks promoting clients' sense of hope?

Having hesitation and doubt are characteristics of substance abusers. It was observed that the participants were resistant to have these kinds of activities. This might be owing to a lack of a sense of security or locus of control. The concept of "challenge by choice" was employed by offering choices and counselling sessions for the participants to decide whether to join the activities or not. No matter what their decisions were, they needed to be supported.

Berman and Davis-Berman (2002:307) recognised that "some adventure programming may create unacceptable high levels of anxiety to clients". This is a real situation existing in Hong Kong adventure practices. AC has become a main methodology for many youth projects in the past decade. However, there is not much systematic training with a clinical basis for AC practitioners or trainers. Many hard skills trainers act as AC facilitators or counsellors. They are not familiar with the conceptual framework, process, programming, skills and techniques for AC. They may adapt military training, boot camp training, methods from disciplinary training camps, or elements from the television show "Survivors" in their AC programmes. Some counsellors even force participants to complete some high events such as abseiling, challenge courses or night walks without considering their psychological state or applying the important concept of "challenge by choice" to their clients (Schoel *et al.*, 1988). Worst still, some workers make use of the high events elements as a tool for discipline or revenge on participants' disturbing behaviours. This act leads to cases of abuse! We question whether risk alone promotes growth?

Nichols (1999) identified that, by using risk constructively together with long-term intensive support, caring, and being sensitive to clients' various needs, counsellors could bring positive outcomes to their clients by improving their self-esteem and promoting their self-responsibility. Clients' personal growth comes from trust, encouragement, fun, comfort, security, and an acceptance in tackling adventure or real-life risks. Berman and Davis-Berman (2002) pointed out that there is a paradigm shift in AC programming, that the AC counsellor should reduce the "perception of risk" in the programme. Instead, the counsellor should "take care of basic needs, work within comfort zone, learn to assess and intervene, and build a therapeutic relationship with the participants" (Berman and David-Berman, 2002:309).

Issue of Authority

The majority of female substance abusers would like to take two to three bowls of rice for every meal. What is the meaning of this act to them? It seems that they were addicted to eating in the hostels! They were eating too much as if there were out of control. Many drug treatment hostels are highly controlled and guarded by staff. Moreover, participants' behaviour is highly supervised and monitored, and staff has the intention of controlling clients' behaviour—for example, staff setting rules and regulations for managing clients' eating issues, such as how many meals per day and how much they could take. However, these rules and regulations make clients feel insecure and worried about hunger, since they perceive that there is no choice allowed to them. Thus, clients take as much as they can for each meal in order to ease their anxiety. It is common for clients to gain weight (e.g. from 80 lbs to 140 lbs) within a month or two. This attempt to control clients cannot help the clients establish self-esteem and self-control. Instead, it just enhances the clients' "sense of inadequacy, helplessness, isolation, and unworthiness" (Beck *et al.*, 1993:250–1). The main goal of the AC group was to allow the group members to police themselves and to attempt to work out their own problems without interference from outside (Glass and Myers, 2001). In other words, the main aim of the AC group process is to facilitate clients in regaining a sense of self-control and self-responsibility for themselves (Beck *et al.*, 1993; Cross, 2002).

Importance of Personal Growth

The treatment goal of substance abusers should focus on facilitating clients in establishing and maintaining a responsible lifestyle (Beck *et al.*, 1993). Some frontline workers have shared their experiences in treating the problematic issues of their clients. The treatment might not help the clients or may even make them worse, because abusive behaviour might be transformed into other abusive forms of behaviour, such as gambling, alcoholism, or sex addiction. It is believed that personal growth should be the ultimate treatment goal for substance abusers.

AC programming is a good tool for facilitating clients' personal growth by improving clients' self-concepts (Berman and Davis-Berman, 2005). Moreover, nurturing clients' resiliency in terms of Belongingness, Competence, and Optimism through an AC programme could help clients to "bounce back" in case of life adversity (Choi *et al.*, 2003). This is the groundwork for substance abuse treatment. The following life stories again help to illustrate the impact of adventure intervention on those young female abusers.

Magic moment

On a February morning, still cool yet warm at times, after having a good night's sleep, 11 female ex-substance abusers began another day of training right after breakfast. They had gone through teamwork training the previous day through various challenging tasks, aiming at polishing their group communication, stretching their ability to express and adapt, igniting the group spirit, as well as enhancing their sense of competence. Among them, some were more active, while some were basically passive. Some tended to express themselves, while some always kept quiet. Some felt at ease during the training, while some took a long time to get involved. Some took the lead, while some were inclined to follow suit. Was it because of the ways they grew up in their families? Were these behaviours the consequences of substance abuse that influenced their self-image and self-confidence? Were these behaviours the side-effects of long-term residential care? Could the challenges in the camp really help to draw out the best in them? The way they might change could be influenced by the atmosphere of the camp, having a break from the hostel routines, or the life-force bursting from the simulated activities.

Eleven girls needed to undertake another challenge: "Challenge Pole". After putting on the safety harness, each of the girls took turns to climb up the 20-feet pole by herself, standing on its top on a small platform virtually without any support, facing a big plastic ball (signifying their personal goals) far ahead. At the end, they were invited to jump out to smash the ball.

The adventure activities challenged their courage and determination. They were encouraged to face the fear coming from the outside environment as well as from within, stepping out of their comfort zone. By setting up their own personal goals, they were guided in learning that the path to goal achievement included personal striving and support from their companions. Perhaps owing to the aftermath of substance abuse, one participant, Ling (a make-up name), was a bit slow in reacting during the activity process. She was quiet and passive, so that even her team-mates described her as such. It seemed that she just didn't care much about participating and achieving. Finally, it was Ling's turn to go up the Challenge Pole.

After the success of the previous team-mates, the whole team (including Ling) had become elated. When she made her declaration, she said with determination: "I declare to get rid of substance abuse, and stay with my son. Will you support me?", the whole team was touched by her genuineness, and said out loudly: "We will support you!"

When Ling climbed up to the top of the pole, her feet trembled and her face was distorted with fear. Underneath the pole, the other girls kept on cheering and encouraging her. After almost half an hour, the worker reminded her about her declaration made earlier and encouraged her to step forward, which then became the driving force, and the worker called to her to persevere and break through. Suddenly, she gathered all her strength, standing upright on the small platform, staring at the ball ahead, calling out loudly: "I want to be with my son!" Then she jumped out and smashed the ball with all her might! After being lowered down, her face beamed with satisfaction, while all the girls embraced her, extending their heartfelt congratulations! A girl standing nearby whispered to his friend: "Wow! She really had the guts to jump out! I really admire her, I wouldn't dare to try if it was me!"

Ling's performance really touched the girls there, and they began to think of her differently. With her goal in mind, disregarding the threat of height and the preconception of her team-mates, together with dogged determination, she stood up fearlessly, stepping out to meet her goal successfully. Surely, life influences life. Ling's genuineness and determination to jump really touched the hearts of all her team-mates!

In order to help them, the first step is the building up of rapport, then designing tailor-made training programmes with the AC approach, and enhancing their instinctual abilities. On the other hand, through communal and spiritual intervention, the worker needs to provide appropriate counselling and emotional support, encouraging them to break through their own psychological barriers. Furthermore, it is through the support from, and identification with, the community, that they are encouraged to renew their self-understanding and to re-plan their future.

Ling could have been the one to be disregarded yet her personal breakthrough served as a source of encouragement to others. To catch a glimpse of this kind of magic moment among the young female substance abusers, the worker needs to enter into their hearts and to understand their needs, especially those with special concerns, such as their beloved children. This genuine caring towards their children can somehow be transformed into inner energy, and become the determination to quit substance abuse and the willingness to change. Henceforth, understanding the family background of the clients, especially the familial relationship, is crucial to the detoxification process. With suitable adventure intervention, the girls can then be spurred to step out from their comfort zone, take the first step into the unknown, enter into the new experience, and ultimately break the bondage of life!

Dynamic Counselling

June (a make-up name), aged 20, was the only child in her family. Her parents died when she was still young, and she was then forced to live with her relatives, and others had always bullied her. When she had grown up, June had developed a strong sense self-protection, being apathetic with others and untrusting, and being hypersensitive to others' dislike and rejection. Ending up as a substance abuser, June was required by the court to receive a one-year residential detoxification treatment programme, where it was arranged for her to join the adventure counselling training programme. During the training, with her proactive participation, as agreed by other members, June became the leader, together with another girl called Yan (a make-up name).

In an orienteering programme, June happened to be in the same group as Yan. While all the members did try their best to participate in the activity, owing to their (June's and Yan's) different views in route planning and map reading, they just couldn't reach a consensus. Consequently, the group atmosphere became tense, the trip was delayed, and at the end they didn't manage to be the first group. After the activity, they were so emotional that they refused to talk about the incident. Two days later when June had calmed down, the worker came to talk to her. June said openly that she felt rejected by others as a slow walker; the team also distrusted her judgement in map and compass usage. Upon further probing, she said, "no one likes to walk with a slow walker, they consider me to be a burden! Why don't they trust the direction I suggest? They don't even listen!" When the worker tried to help her identify similar experiences of being rejected in the past, tears swelled up in her eyes. Her emotions of not being accepted, not being trusted, as well as the sense of rejection in the past were aroused. "Those who love me died. There is no true love in this world!" June sobbed. The relentless desire for love and the wound created by her parents' death were there. She was helped to released her emotion. Later, June was invited to speak with Yan, expressing her own feelings, as well as apologising for the inflicted hurt on Yan. They got to know each other more and were reconciled.

In another camping activity, the two girls cooperated with each other well. While June was struggling when hiking with a heavy rucksack, Yan took the initiative to share her load. During the debriefing time, both of them showed their appreciation to the group members. June expressed, "My group members really treat me so good!" In a loving environment, one can trust and be trusted. A sure and genuine smile shone on June's face again. With the gentle warmth overflowing in the community, it seemed that the wound within was fading!

Conclusion

As a developing model, adventure counselling has been widely used in Hong Kong. However, among all those organisations providing services for young female substance abusers, the use of adventure counselling is still limited to a few of them, serving as a pilot programme or supplementary intervention. While the girls tended to think that they could not do anything to cope with life stress and to resist the lure of addiction, adventure counselling can serve to create successful experiences in a group setting, to confront negative automatic thoughts, to change distorted thinking, and to teach functional coping mechanisms.

Since the girls tended to have a strong sense of emotional attachment and dependence, the group-learning setting helped to provide the necessary warmth, support and healthy boundary for surviving the initial stage. Furthermore, it is only through trust within the group that the girls dared to step out from their personal comfort zone and try out new ways to live. Furthermore, the proactive culture in the group, as well as the authentic life model of the counsellors, gave a sense of hope to the participants, believing that everyone can achieve their personal goals someday, and that if other members can do it, they can do it too!

In fact, rather than purely tender loving care, it is the high and meaningful expectation that helps to build up the girls' motivation to become good. Trusting that they can always move one small step at a time, it is the artful balance of challenge and competence, as well as the continuous step-by-step training that allow the girls to taste peak experiences, to feel the joy of satisfaction and to be transformed by the educational moments during the process. Knowing that the girls might either become explosive or retreat into depression in the midst of the challenges and pressure, on-the-spot counselling with the supplement of medication, if needed, would prevent the girls going from bad to worse. It is a common experience that, no matter how bad it might be, that experience can serve as the basis of learning and personal growth upon timely intervention.

Moreover, for effective intervention, adventure counselling needs to work with other interventions provided by the organisation, such as teaching, counselling, residential living, work experience, etc. Furthermore, besides preparing the girls physically and psychologically before joining the adventure counselling programme, it is aimed to help the girls to put anything that they have learnt from the programme into real-life practice. Choosing to employ the adventure counselling approach to serve the young female substance abusers is in itself an adventure into the wilderness. It is tough, but it can help the girls by drawing out their best, calling out their dreams and living out their beauty!

References

Beard, C., and Wilson, J. P. (2002). *The Power of Experiential Learning: A Handbook for Trainers and Educators*. London: Kogan Page.

Beck, A. T., Wright, F. D., Newman, C. F., and Liese, B. S. (1993). *Cognitive Therapy of Substance Abuse*. New York: The Guilford Press.

Beringer A. (2004). "Towards an Ecological Paradigm in Adventure Programme," *Journal of Experimental Education, Volume 27 (1)*, pp. 51–66.

Berman, D. S., and Davis-Berman, J. (2002). "Risk and Anxiety in Adventure Programming," *Journal of Experiential Education, Volume 25 (2)*, pp. 305–310.

Berman, D. S., and Davis-Berman, J. (2005). "Positive Psychology and Outdoor Education," *Journal of Experiential Education, Volume 28 (1)*, pp. 17–24.

Cartwright, A. (1987). "Group Work with Substance Abusers: Basic Issues and Future Research," *British Journal of Addiction, Volume 82*, pp. 951–953.

Caulkins, M. C., White, D. D., and Russell, K. C. (2006). "The Role of Physical Exercise in Wilderness Therapy for Troubled Adolescent Women," *Journal of Experiential Education, Volume 29 (1)*, pp. 18–37.

Cheung, C. K., Lee, T. Y., and Lee, C. M. (2003). "Factors in Successful Relapse Prevention among Hong Kong Drug Addicts," *Journal of Offender Rehabilitation, Volume 37 (3/4)*, pp. 179–199.

Choi, P., and *et al.* (2003). *Fostering Resilient Youth: Practical Handbook for Families and Schools*. Hong Kong: Breakthrough Ltd. (in Chinese)

Coady, N. F. and Wolgien, C. S. (1996). "Good Therapists' View of How They are Helpful," *Clinical Social Work Journal, Volume 24 (3)*, pp. 333–22.

Cross, R. (2002). "The Effects of an Adventure Education Program on Perceptions of Alienation and Personal Control among At-risk Adolescents," *Journal of Experiential Education, Volume 25 (1)*, pp. 247–254.

Edwards, J. K., and Bess, J. M. (1998). "Developing Effectiveness in the Therapeutic Use of Self," *Clinical Social Work Journal, Volume 26 (1)*, pp. 89–105.

Fletcher, T. B., and Hinkle, J. S. (2002). "Adventure Based Counselling: An Innovation in Counselling," *Journal of Counselling & Development, Volume 80*, pp. 277–285.

Glass, J. S., and Myers, J. E. (2001). "Combining the Old and the New to Help Adolescents: Individual Psychology and Adventure-based Counselling," *Journal of Mental Health Counselling, Volume 23 (2)*, pp. 104–114.

Itin, C. M. (2001). "Adventure Therapy—Critical Questions," *Journal of Experiential Education, Volume 24 (2)*, pp. 80–84.

Kivlighan, D. M., and Holmes, S. E. (2004). "The Importance of Therapeutic Factors: A Typology of Therapeutic Factors Studies," In *Handbook of Group Counselling and Psychotherapy*, edited by J. L. Delucra-Waak, D. A. Gerrity, C. R. Kalodner, and M. T. Riva, pp. 23–36. London: Sage.

Lau, J. (2003). *Report on Evaluation of the Understanding the Adolescent Project (UAP) in Secondary Schools 2001/02*. Hong Kong: The Chinese University of Hong Kong. Centre for Clinical Trials and Epidemiological Research School of Public Health.

Lee, T. S., and Mak, S. W. (2002). *Adventure Counselling Handbook*. Hong Kong: Breakthrough Ltd. (in Chinese)

Narcotics Division (2006). *Central Registry of Drug Abuse: Fifty-four Report*. Hong Kong: Narcotics Division, Security Bureau, Government of the Hong Kong Special Administrative Region.

Narcotics Division. (n.d.) *Central Registry of Drug Abuse*. (Retrieved on 1 April 2007), www.nd.gov.hk.

Neff, J. A., and MacMaster, S. A. (2005). "Apply Behavior Change Models to Understand Spiritual Mechanisms Underlying Change in Substance Abuse Treatment," *The American Journal of Drug and Alcohol, Volume 31*, pp. 669–684.

Nichols, G. (1999). "Is Risk a Valuable Component of Outdoor Adventure Programmes for Young Offenders undergoing Drug Rehabilitation?" *Journal of Youth Studies, Volume 2 (1)*, pp. 101–115.

Ng, H. Y. (1999). *Beliefs and Therapeutic Change: A Study of Approach to Drug Rehabilitation*. (Unpublished doctoral dissertation) Hong Kong: Chinese University of Hong Kong.

Persons, J. B. (1989). *Cognitive Therapy in Practice: A Case Formulation Approach*. New York: W. W. Norton & Company.

Priest, S. and Gass, M. A. (1997). *Effective Leadership in Adventure Programming*. U.S.A.: Human Kinetics.

Prouty, D. (1990). "Project Adventure: A Brief History," In *Adventure Education*, edited by J. C. Miles and S. Priest, pp. 99–109. State College: Venture Publishing, Inc.

Russell, K. C. (2001). "What is Wilderness Therapy?" *Journal of Experiential Education, Volume 24 (2)*, pp. 70–79.

Russell, K. C., and Phillips-Miller, D. (2002). "Perspectives on the Wilderness Therapy Process and its Relation to Outcome," *Child & Youth Care Forum, Volume 31 (6)*, pp. 415–437.

Satir, V. (1987). "The Therapist Story," In *The Use of Self in Therapy*, edited by M. Baldwin and V. Satir, pp. 17–25. New York: Haworth.

Schoel, J., Prouty, D., and Radcliffe, P. (1988). *Islands of Healing: A Guide to Adventure Based Counselling*. Hamilton: Project Adventure.

Seligman, M. E. P., Walker, E. F., and Rosenhan, D. L. (2001). *Abnormal Psychology. (4th edition)* New York: W. W. Norton & Company.

Ward, D. E., and Litchy, M. (2004). "The Effective Use of Processing in Groups," In *Handbook of Group Counselling and Psychotherapy*, edited by J. L. Delucra-Waak, D. A. Gerrity, C. R. Kalodner, and M. T. Riva, pp. 104–119. London: Sage.

Weiss, R. D., Jaffee, W. B., Menil, V. P., and Cogley, C. B. (2004). "Group Therapy for Substance Use Disorders: What do We Know?" *Harvard Review Psychiatry, Volume 12 (6)*, pp. 339–350.

Yalom, I. D. (2002). *The Gift of Therapy: An Open Letter to a New Generation of Therapists and their Patients*. New York: Harper Collins Publishers Inc.

Yalom, I. D., and Leszcz M. (2005). *The Theory and Practice of Group Psychotherapy. (5th edition)* New York: Basic Books.

WORKING WITH YOUTH IN SOCIAL WITHDRAWAL

8

Victor Cheong-wing WONG

Introduction

The phenomenon of youth-at-risk, who are socially withdrawn from social interactions with peers, and disengaged from education, training and employment, has recently aroused much public and professional concern, particularly after the broadcast of a local television documentary in early 2005. Three years previously in 2002, a BBC documentary on the magnitude of the Japanese phenomenon of "hikikomori" (a term coined by psychologist Dr. Tamaki Saito, with the literal meaning of pulling away and being confined) alarmed the western world to the existence of a very vulnerable, yet invisible group of young hermits. The causes of "hikikomori" in Japan are argued to be culturally and nationally specific (Dziesinski, 2003). However it may be a tendency that is emerging in other societies characterised by very keen competition and increasing risks at both social and economic levels. Even the most casual search of Internet materials will show that the same phenomenon is reported worldwide, East and West.

In order to come up with a better understanding of the phenomenon of social withdrawal, one must arrive at some consensus as to what the core indicators of social withdrawal are. The term "indicators," rather than "symptoms," is preferred, as the latter tends to downplay the social and structural forces that shape the development and course of social withdrawal, and tends to overemphasise individual deficits and pathologise the psychological make-up of individuals (Golden *et al.*, 2002). However, the use of the term "indicators" cannot guarantee to do away the individualising of young people's risks and problems and the pathologising of their characters, if mere behavioural problems or indicators are employed. It is against this background that this chapter adopts the social exclusion perspective in order that the relationship between personal withdrawal or exclusion experience and the social context can be better understood.

Social withdrawal may cause nothing harmful or dangerous if it is done for just a short period of time. For example, it is not unusual for healthy persons to engage in the state of solitude for the purpose of meditation or just for taking a break from burdensome work and stressful social relations (Scott, 2002). However without a clear or legitimate purpose and with a period lasting very long, social withdrawal may finally end up entrapping the individual. So, in the definition of social withdrawal, both the temporal dimension and personal meanings attached to the reclusion experience should be addressed.

There is so far only one social work team in Hong Kong specialising in providing outreach and engagement services to these vulnerable youth who happen to shut themselves into rooms without any participation in social institutions, and do not have any interactions with others for an incredibly long period of time. As a consultant of this challenging new project, the author, together with the supervisor of the project, conducted a small-scale research study on the users' profile and the service tactics and strategies employed by the team (Wong and Ying, 2006). In light of the theoretical perspective of social exclusion and with reference to the study, the initiatives and tactics of serving this particular group of youth-at-risk are discussed.

Theoretical Perspective: Social Exclusion

As a multi-dimensional process, social exclusion is defined as a failure of social integration, in which various forms of exclusion are combined, such as exclusion from participation in decision-making, access to training or employment opportunities and material resources, and integration into common cultural processes (Burchardt, 2000; Hills *et al.*, 2000; Madanipour *et al.*, 1998; Percy-Smith, 2000; Walker and Walker, 1997). But unfortunately, it is observed that so many developed economies in the European Union tend to reduce social integration simply to labour market integration, without addressing the overall trend against young people in many other spheres of life (Walther, 2006). This is not to deny the importance of young people's exclusion from and integration into the labour market, but its relationship to other spheres of youth transitions into adulthood must also be taken into account, including family, housing, partnerships, careers, commitment, political participation and lifestyle. There are at least three levels of social exclusion that need to be thoroughly addressed if social inclusion and re-engagement are to be realised, namely, institutional, cultural and relational.

At the institutional level, apart from work or employment, education and training also matter, and they are taken as the three major social institutions in accounting for the school-to-work transition (Coles, 1995). The idea of "Status Zero" is used to describe those young people who are not in education, employment or training (NEET), and who cannot enjoy a legitimate social status in their search for a transitional pathway to adulthood, for they are neither students nor trainees/workers themselves (Williamson, 1997). That is, other than being perceived as junior citizens or the younger generation, they do not enjoy any legitimate social status in regard to their position in society at large. If everything is reduced to personal deficits, young people are merely the ones to be blamed for their lack of skills, knowledge, qualifications, attitude and readiness to take up all the challenges in their transitions. The social exclusion perspective has shed light on the role played by social policy and social institutions in blaming the victims, excluding the disadvantaged youth groups, justifying unequal access to and stratification of the youth labour market, and perpetuating the mismatch and gaps between education/training and the labour market (Chiu, 2005; Chiu and Wong, 2000; Wong and Shiu, 2003). Given the reality of fractured youth transitions and differential access to education, training and the labour market, the forces of social exclusion have to be well examined if the problems experienced by the disadvantaged and vulnerable young people are not to be individualised and atomised (Coles, 1997; Helve, 1997; Todman, 2004; Wong, 2004).

Exclusion in the cultural sphere may take place if young people cannot enjoy access to tangible financial means and intangible social support in a world of youth consumption that has been increasingly commodified (Besley, 2003; UNESCO, 2003; Wyn and White, 1997). Having experienced institutional and cultural exclusion, disengaged young people would not pay so much attention to style and body management, or even to personal hygiene, and may develop a different style of living and culture that mainstream people and society at large find difficult to accept (Chiu and Wong, 2000).

There is no doubt that social exclusion is also a personal story experienced at the intra- and inter-personal levels. Young people suffering from traumas or failures may be filled with personal frustrations and despair that finally lead to the behaviour of social withdrawal. The situation of "social isolates" (Adler and Adler, 1996), who have very limited ties with peers and a decrease in social interaction with others, may lead to disengagement from the concerns of others. Individual factors do count, but the withdrawal and unavailability of social support on the part of society may further perpetuate the social isolation and exclusion experience of individuals. It is within this context that social exclusion comes into play and the spiral of perpetuation may not be well addressed unless more pro-active approaches like home visits and engagement services can be provided. Moreover, on the interpersonal level, young people experiencing social exclusion may be deprived of any meaningful social relations with peers, friends, and adults (Julkunen, 2001). Social exclusion taking the form of discrimination, rejection, isolation or bullying undesirably leads to the piling up of personal frustrations, poor social skills, loneliness, anxiety, etc. In view of this, and in view of the lack of social support, social withdrawal may be taken as the last resort to prevent any further teasing and bullying from taking place. But chronic social withdrawal paradoxically reduces the social isolates' ability to develop social relations with others and even to develop a sense of reality (Csikszentmihalyi, 1997).

Screening Indicators and Efforts for Identifying Social Withdrawal Cases

As discussed, social withdrawal may be productive and positive if it is taken for just a short period of time for re-energising, or for a longer period of solitude for the purpose of personal reflection, productive disengagement or the completion of a meaningful task. As far as help seeking is concerned, we cannot afford to overlook the centrality of personal meaning and the temporal dimension. Otherwise, professional intervention may end up as a means of social control that would lead to discrimination and stigmatization. To minimise the labelling effect, the term social withdrawal is not directly translated into an adjective describing this disadvantaged group in wordings like "socially withdrawn" youth. The reason behind this is to create a gap or distance between social withdrawal and young people, for they maybe one day tune in again to mainstream life, and young people may be able, with self-determination or with the help of others, to fight against social withdrawal and the undesirable impact caused. Most importantly, more space is created for practitioners to avoid developing an individualist discourse around the phenomenon, and to adopt a more critical perspective in examining the underlying structural causes of the problem. Social work practitioners need to address both the personal and structural dimensions of social withdrawal in regard to the screening in and out of potential cases.

One of the important indicators that social workers would like to pay special attention to is self-enquiry made by potential clients who can share over the phone their despair or frustration as a result of the long-term entrapment caused by social withdrawal. Another important indicator is the duration of social withdrawal which happens to last on average two years, as far as the pool of users served by the team is concerned (Hong Kong Christian Service, 2007). In the case of Japan, academics and practitioners used a six-month period as the temporal indicator of "hikikomori." However, for the sake of earlier prevention or intervention, the idea of using three months as the threshold in defining the temporal dimension is now seriously under consideration in Japan (Dziesinski, 2003).

Another necessary, but not sufficient, indicator in defining social withdrawal is the social-exclusion experience of young people who are excluded, isolated or withdrawn from participating in the three major social institutions discussed above. What needs to be emphasised is that, in many cases, youth belonging to the NEET group (or NEET youth) are not necessarily social withdrawals if they still keep in touch with their friends in spite of their lack of social legitimacy as students, workers or trainees. In other words, social withdrawals are mostly NEET youth simultaneously, but not necessarily vice versa. In some cases where students have not yet officially left schools, but have been absent from classes for a long period of time, they may be regarded as marginal cases of social withdrawal. In the most severe cases, young people may even be disengaged from interactions with their families in spite of living under the same roof with their parents or other family members.

On the level of interpersonal relationships, young people may want to interact with their friends but paradoxically avoid them because they fear that they will be negatively evaluated and bullied. As far as the relational dimension is concerned, social withdrawals are excluded or withdrawn from having any face-to-face interactions with peers, and feel insecure in social relationships. In a world characterised by the increasing popularity of the use of the Internet, young people confined to social withdrawal may opt to be engaged in virtual communication and interaction with others over the Internet, which can be interpreted as an outcry of their desire to get connected with humans and with the outside world at large, in spite of their hesitation, reluctance and difficulty in stepping outside their rooms or flats into the real world.

The use of the screening indicators discussed above is deemed important not only on the grounds of service targeting, but also for making the most of available resources, particularly in view of the labour- and time-intensive nature of the service on the one hand, and the lack of continuing public funding support on the other hand. According to figures from the team, in the period between 1 November 2005 and 31 December 2006, a total number of 986 persons made telephone enquiries concerning this specific service targeted on young withdrawals. After screening and filtering, about one-fifth (19.5%) or 192 of the potential clients were taken as cases for follow-up actions (Hong Kong Christian Service, 2007).

Unlike the Japanese counterparts who are mostly of middle-class background, most of the cases (95%) outreached by the team were of working-class background, which can be taken as a powerful explanation of the materiality of social exclusion. But there is one thing similar in the two societies, and that is that most of the withdrawals in both places are males rather than females (Wong and Ying, 2006). As reflected in the updated figures supplied by the team (Hong Kong Christian Service, 2007), male clients constitute more than four-fifths (81.3%) of the cases served. Unlike their "anti-social" counterparts, who are the targets of outreach social workers, social isolates are usually free of any criminal records. Among all the 192 cases, there were only two cases who were cautioned under the Police Superintendent's Discretion Scheme.

Service Tactics and Strategies

Upon receiving hot-line telephone enquiries, and collecting further information from the enquirers, be they self-referrals, referrals from family, relatives or peers, or referrals from support professionals or the formal sector, the team engages in deliberate case-discussion according to the screening criteria discussed above, and decide whether to take any cases and begin the outreach actions. Unlike conventional youth outreach work which takes place in the streets, housing estate playgrounds and corners, karaoke boxes, commercial arcades, and other public or private places, efforts made by the team are in the form of home visits to the clients. Overall, there are two major phases of work apart from the initial phase of telephone enquiries and case screening, namely, rapport building and engagement work, which form the focus of this section respectively.

Rapport Building and Initial Working Relationship

Rapport building with the parents and the clients, in particular, is the first and essential phase of the outreach work in the form of home visits. For example, the practitioners, who usually go in pairs, ask the parents and the sons or daughters if it is possible to share their family photos and past stories (Hong Kong Christian Service, 2006). This can help highlight the unique outcome of mutuality of family support, particularly when the good old days are being excluded from the collective memories of the family. Even in the absence of the child's involvement in telling the beautiful stories, which is conducive to the promotion of a more peaceful atmosphere that has long been lost in the family, it is trusted that the client could still overhear what was being told beyond the room. Such a practice is indeed in line with therapeutic interventions informed by poststructuralist perspectives, such as solution-focused and narrative therapies where exceptions and sparkling moments are taken as counter-themes or plots for exploring life alternatives (de Shazer and Berg, 1992; White and Epston, 1990). In case either one or both of the parents were arguing with, blaming or scolding the client, the two workers would assume a division of labour with one talking with the parent(s), and the other talking with the user on an individual basis. The practitioners prefer to talk with the parents about their worries, frustrations or anger concerning their child in the absence of the client, rather than reproducing the usual scenarios of parent-child conflicts.

Another important principle for the practitioners to follow is to start from where the clients are, particularly in relation to their strengths and interests, like observing and talking about their current hobbies and activities which are given time and space for fuller description. What needs to be demystified is the idea that the sharing of their interests and activities like Internet chatting and game playing may only end up further encouraging young people entrapped in social withdrawal, but without taking the courage to face the real world in terms of going back to schools or going out to find jobs. In some extreme cases, some parents and even some practitioners believe in the use of "shock therapy" in the sense of unplugging the computer cable to stop the young from virtualising the real world (Berger, 2002; Pais, 2000), without noticing that the computer or Internet space could be used the other way round for boosting their morale and energy, and for connecting with others or realizing the virtual world (Besley, 2003; Cockburn, 2005; Livingstone and Bober, 2004; Valkenburg and Soeters, 2001). Being entrapped in social withdrawal year after year, what is most needed is to re-establish the clients' self-confidence and their trust in others, rather than educating them in a wiser use of the Internet, unless and until they have such an agenda in mind. Use of Internet chatting or SMS, whether simultaneous or not, can be taken as a means of connecting or re-connecting with others at their own pace. The team has set up a specific website where young people and their clients can easily get access to the agency anytime they like, and the practitioners are eager to pass on to the clients their own email addresses and office telephone numbers for contact. Of course, response on the side of practitioners is a must. But it is not unusual that the clients may stop responding to the practitioners over the phone or Internet, or even to resist to be visited at home. The process of rapport building or initial working relationship with social withdrawals is not linear or progressive in nature. What is most needed is not only skills, but also the concern, patience and consistency of the practitioners.

To promote the change of personal motivation, interventions, facilities and programmes have to be tailor-made to individual interests as far as possible. In the beginning phase, a client's room or home is usually an ideal place for conversations and activities, by bearing in mind that the space outside is still alien to or of no interest to the clients (Hong Kong Christian Service, 2006).

Innovative means that can be employed in the phase of initial working relationship building include, but are not restricted to, celebrating festivals or a client's birthday at home, eating together at a client's home or, if possible, in a canteen or restaurant within the nearby community, inviting peer counsellors to share with or teach clients any areas of interest they like, etc. (Wong and Ying, 2006). Generation of subjective interest, combined with a sequence of personal involvement in interest-driven activities, should be made possible both in tangible and intangible senses (Lens, Sheldon and Deci, 2004). Without developing a sense of intrinsic motivation, it may be premature to join any existing pre-vocational or training package, as this may reproduce another cycle of frustration not favourable for relationship building and engagement work.

Users' daily living which is constantly disrupted by social withdrawal and social exclusion has to be handled with care. The institutional logic of inclusion places much emphasis on the discourse of employability, but without addressing individual preference and interest which has to be reassessed (Walther, 2006), as the clients may still be resistant to any premature institutional re-engagement. Fully acknowledging and flexibly supporting the interests and activities of clients are not only effective means in better cementing the helping relationship, but are also keys to understanding the clients' strengths that can be gradually transformed for the purpose of breaking through the vicious cycle of social withdrawal.

Engagement Work

After existing in the state of social withdrawal for a long time, the clients may find it difficult to cope with any new engagement experience. For example, in interacting with other young people in training programmes offered by the agency, a few clients were teased and labelled as socially withdrawn guys, and as a result, they withdrew from initial re-engagement with others on the relational level. Young people are characterised by diversity and heterogeneity, and mutual exclusion may be perpetuated if the label of social withdrawal is not critically demystified. After further work and encouragement, it was good to see that three clients, who did not know each other previously, were willing to step out of their cocoons and share their experiences with others in a programme organised by the team. Probably because of having the same background of suffering from social withdrawal, they could enjoy chatting together and made friends later on. Within the three-member group, a female youth shared with two other male youth her web-posted diary, receiving a listening ear. In return, the girl gave support to one of the two boys being interviewed by the media about his social withdrawal experience. From this story we can see that practitioners need to provide an atmosphere which is conducive to clients' interaction with one another; but at the end it still depends on the informal interaction among the clients themselves.

There are three things that we can observe from this, the first of which is the non-linearity of relational re-engagement, the second is the importance of the recognition and acknowledgement of the cultural practice of young people, for example, sharing of a web-posted diary, and the third is the appreciation of the informal dimension or informality of engagement. Whether the component of informal learning and participation can be bridged with formal learning opportunities is surely one of the challenges which policy makers and practitioners need to confront in the days ahead (du Bois-Reymond, 2003). In order to support the clients in having a real taste for going back to school, and experiencing a short period of job-trial, for example, the team has to make much effort in lobbying supportive schools and sympathetic employers to give the clients flexible or alternative arrangements tailor-made to their specific needs.

Another case-example is a male user aged 18 who had grown up in one of the outlying islands of Hong Kong. He did not leave his home except for going to the barber shop for a haircut twice a year for three years. He woke up everyday between 6 p.m. to 9 p.m., and then began to read Chinese history books, watch TV and listen to an evening radio programme hosted by his idol. Other than these activities he would remain idle at home for the rest of the day. The reason for his decision to hide himself at home was that, ever since he was promoted to Secondary 1, he was unable to adapt to life in the secondary school and had been suffering from stress.

The island is just a relatively small community with pretty close neighbouring relations. His situation was widely known by everybody, and for this reason he did not want to go out, but rather, kept himself away from the eyes and gossip of the neighbours. He wanted to leave the island and look for a job in the city, but without success. Gradually, he got used to staying at home. Upon watching the TV programme "Sunday Documentary" on the topic of social withdrawal of young people in Hong Kong, he made the move to phone for assistance as he feared that he might have become one of them.

Before helping the boy to re-enter the community, the social worker had to assist him by building up his trust so as to expand his security net which was needed to regain courage. Therefore, it was most important for the social worker to feel and understand what the young man wanted, while showing concern for his needs. Connecting to the community through tangible support, the boy was gradually able to get familiar with and understand the external world which had been excluded from his world for three years. Taking the opportunity of identity-card application, he was accompanied and shown how his interests can match his needs in a tour that explored the many places he wished to go. Through the community resource of the Hong Kong Central Library, the boy learned how to search for job vacancies via surfing the Labour Department website. This certainly reinforced his relation with the society.

Meanwhile, creating a natural environment for the client to revisit the external world and guiding him on a tour all helped to enhance his sense of security in rejoining as a member of the community. He was also offered a trip to Central District to take photos, inspiring his interests in history and to explore with him the good and bad things caused by the change of the city. Throughout the process, the presence of positive feelings and pleasant memories are of vital importance. For instance, with trusting and safe working-relations, the boy was accompanied to a book shop and encouraged to search for his favourite history books. While staying inside the City Hall Public Library, he could analyse and compare the old and new buildings of the Legislative Council and the Bank of China that represent the change of the eras. Both activities were based on his own interests: history and news events. Matching his personal interests with recognition of the real world, and finding the way to integrate into the community, the client, through his own efforts, had succeeded in finding a job in a newspaper advertisement. He is now working as a chef in a chain fast-food shop.

The road to re-engagement is not linear, but complex, which is characterised by ups and downs, and with steps forward and steps backward, just like the case of youth transition from school to work (Walther *et al.*, 2002). To help young people face the discrimination in the dominant society and small communities, we not only need the help of social workers but, most importantly, we need society at large to recognise the difficulties, desires and values of youth in their transition, and thus adapting the relative systems to match. This includes the exercise of institutional flexibility and tolerance, and the promotion of peer-group and community acceptance, coupled with well-designed and tailor-made services allowing room for individual manoeuvring, which can help the clients to recognise and develop their own trajectory differently and divergently from the so-called normal pathway.

Challenges Ahead

As the service is skill-demanding and time-consuming, one of the key challenges ahead is to involve the end users as much as possible. For example, for those clients who have successfully overcome the state of social isolation and re-entered the community or society as students or workers, they may be invited to have interaction and conversations with those clients who still stay or hide at home and who are entrapped in social withdrawal, or with those clients who are in the process of community re-engagement. With the back-up of support and training provided by the practitioners and the agency, the involvement of the youth mentors or volunteers will prove to be a "win-win" scenario to all parties concerned.

Another critical challenge is to involve and support the clients' parents throughout the whole intervention process in spite of the heavy workload caused by direct work with the clients. Living under the same roof with their child, the parents are the victims of the phenomenon of social withdrawal as well. In many cases, parents are not free from reproducing the institutional logic of inclusion in the sense of hard pressing or "softly" continually encouraging their child to resume a normal way of living, either to continue study, or to seek a job in the labour market. The parents need to be made aware of the negative impact caused by this kind of institutional or mainstream logic, which is in fact a major cause leading to the exclusion and withdrawal experience of their child in the first place. On top of the necessity of deconstructing the institutional logic, the running of groups for parents to acquire new knowledge, ventilate their feelings, share their stories and express their ideas are also important.

Service flexibility is a keyword of social work intervention with this vulnerable group of youth. Yet, the service goal of smoothing or promoting the transition from social withdrawal to social engagement cannot be realised simply by the efforts made on the part of the agency and practitioners. So, another big challenge ahead is to convey to the community partners—such as schools, employers, training institutions and other community organisations—the purposes and meanings of reaching out and engaging this vulnerable yet invisible group of youth-at-risk and to encourage them to exercise much more discretion and flexibility and, if possible, to input additional resources for the sake of re-engaging the clients.

Through workshops and seminars, social workers working in other youth work settings, such as integrated teams, may be able to learn from their more experienced colleagues the brand-new perspective, skills, knowledge and techniques involved in serving cases of such disadvantaged background. But it should not rule out the strategy that more specialised teams should be established to cater for increasing needs or demands, particularly in view of the growing gaps between the haves and have-nots in the context of Hong Kong. This is a matter of importance and urgency as, so far, the only agency specialising in this new mode of service has not yet been able to receive government funding on a regular basis.

Concluding Remarks

Social withdrawal is a complex social exclusion process demonstrating the interlocking relationship between the subjective and the structural. On the one hand, youth work practitioners have to address the meanings and interpretations young people and their family members attach to the isolation experience and the social context within which this has emerged or been suppressed. On the other hand, practitioners have to make tremendous efforts to mobilise community concern and resources in working with the clients and their parents if the cultural and institutional constraints are to be overcome. Central to rapport building and re-engagement work is the acknowledgement of and support for clients' interests and abilities, and the promotion of interventional and organisational flexibility. Successful transition from the withdrawal stage to the re-engagement scenario is not linear, but dynamic and reversible in nature, which demands patience, skill, and ongoing critical reflections on professional and organisational practices on the part of youth-work practitioners and agencies, and of course the involvement and participation of the clients and their significant others.

Acknowledgements

The author wishes to thank Ms. Winnie Ying and her colleagues in the Life Engagement Training Scheme of Hong Kong Christian Service, and the research funding support from the Hong Kong Baptist University (Grant number: FRG/05-06/I-01).

References

Adler, P. A. and Adler, P. (1996). "Preadolescent Clique Stratification and the Hierarchy of Identity," *Sociological Inquiry, Volume* 66, pp. 11–142.

Berger, A. A. (2002). *Video Games: A Popular Culture Phenomenon.* London: Transaction Publishers.

Besley, T. (2003). "Hybridized and Globalized Youth Cultures in the Postmodern Era," *Review of Education/Pedagogy/Cultural Studies, Volume 25 (2)*, pp. 75–99.

Burchardt, T. (2000). "Social Exclusion: Concepts, and Evidence," In *Breadline Britain: The Measurement of Poverty,* edited by D. Gordon and P. Townsend, pp. 385–405. Bristol: Policy Press.

Chiu, S. (2005). "Rethinking Youth Problems in a Risk Society: Some Reflections on Social Work with Youth-at-Risk in Hong Kong," In *Working with Youth-at-Risk in Hong Kong,* edited by F. Lee, pp. 99–112. Hong Kong: Hong Kong University Press.

Chiu, S. and Wong, V. (2000). "Youth Unemployment in Hong Kong: Constraints and Social Policy Prospects," *Social Policy and Social Work, Volume 4 (2)*, pp. 91–126.

Cockburn, T. (2005). "New Information Communication Technologies and the Development of a Children's Community of Interest," *Community Development Journal*, *Volume 40 (3)*, pp. 329–42.

Coles, B. (1995). *Youth and Social Policy: Youth Citizenship and Young Careers.* London: UCL Press.

Coles, B. (1997). "Vulnerable Youth and Processes of Social Exclusion: A Theoretical Framework, a Review of Recent Research and Suggestions for a Future Research Agenda," In *Youth, Citizenship and Social Change in a European Context*, edited by J. Bynner, L. Chisholm and A. Furlong, pp. 69–88. Aldershot: Ashgate.

Csikszentmihalyi, M. (1997). *Living Well: The Psychology of Everyday Life*. London: Phoenix.

de Shazer, S. and Berg, I. K. (1992). "Doing Therapy: A Post-structural Revision," *Journal of Martial and Family Therapy, Volume 8 (1)*, pp. 71–82.

du Bois-Reymond, M. (2003). *Study on the Links between Formal and Non-formal Education*. Strasbourg: Council of Europe.

Dziesinski, M. J. (2003). *Hikikomori: Investigations into the Phenomenon of Acute Social Withdrawal in Contemporary Japan*. http://towakudai.blogs.com/Hikikomori.Research.Survey.pdf.

Golden, S., Spielhofer, T., Sims, D., Alston, S. and O'Donnell, L. (2002). *Re-engaging the Hardest-to-help Young People: The Role of the Neighbourhood Support Fund*. London: Stationery Office.

Helve, H. (1997). "Perspectives on Social Exclusion, Citizenship and Youth," In *Youth, Citizenship and Social Change in a European Context*, eduted by J.Bynner, L. Chisholm and A. Furlong, pp. 228–233. Aldershot: Ashgate.

Hills, J., Le Grand, J. and Piachaud, D. (eds.) (2000). *Understanding Social Exclusion*. Oxford: Oxford University Press.

Hong Kong Christian Service (2006). *Hidden Messages: Behind the Phenomenon of Social Withdrawal*. Hong Kong: Life Engagement Training Scheme, Hong Kong Christian Service.

Hong Kong Christian Service (2007). *Press Conference Release on the Phenomenon of Social Withdrawal of Young People and the Pressure of the Parents cum Service Effectiveness*. 14 Jan 2007, Hong Kong: Hong Kong Christian Service (in Chinese). www.hkcs.org/news/press/2007press/press20070114.htm.

Julkunen, I. (2001). "Coping and Mental Well-being among Unemployed Youth—A Northern European Perspective," *Journal of Youth Studies, Volume 4 (3)*, pp. 261–278.

Lens, W., Sheldon, K. M. and Deci, E. L. (2004). "Motivating Learning, Performances and Persistence: the Synergistic Effects of Intrinsic Goal Contents and Autonomy-supportive Contexts," *Journal of Personality and Social Psychology, Volume 87 (2)*, pp. 246–260.

Levitas, R. (2000). "What is Social Exclusion?" In *Breadline Europe: The Measurement of Poverty*, edited by R. Levitas, pp. 357–383. Bristol: The Policy Press.

Livingstone, S. and Bober, M. (2004). *UK Children Go Online: Surveying the Experiences of Young People and their Parents.* (Project Report) London: London School of Economics and Political Science. http://eprints.lse.ac.uk/archive/00000395/01/UKCGOsurveyreport.pdf.

Madanipour, A., Cars, G. and Allen, J. (eds.) (1998). *Social Exclusion in European Cities.* London: Jessica Kingsley.

Pais, J. M. (2000). "Transitions and Youth Cultures: Forms and Performances," *International Social Science Journal*, edited by A. Furlong, *Volume 164*, pp. 219–232.

Percy-Smith, J. (2000). "Introduction: The Contours of Social Exclusion," In *Policy Responses to Social Exclusion: Towards Inclusion?* edited by J. Percy-Smith, pp. 1–21. Buckingham: Open University Press.

Scott, D. (2002). *Easy-to-use Zen: Refresh and Calm Your Mind, Body and Spirit with the Wisdom of Zen.* New York: Vega.

Todman, L. C. (2004). *Reflections on Social Exclusion: What Is It? How Is It Different from U.S. Conceptualizations of Disadvantage? And, Why Americans Might Consider Integrating It into U.S. Social Policy Discourse.* City Futures Conference. University of Illinois at Chicago. www.uic.edu/cuppa/cityfutures/papers/webpapers/cityfuturespapers/session23/2_3reflections.pdf.

UNESCO (2003). "Young People in a Globalized World," In *World Youth Report*, edited by UNESCO. Paris: UNESCO.

Valkenburg, P. and Soeters, K. (2001). "Children's Positive and Negative Experiences with the Internet: An Exploratory Study," *Communication Research, Volume 28 (5)*, pp. 652–675.

Walker, A. and Walker, C. (eds.) (1997). *Britain Divided: The Growth of Social Exclusion in the 1980s and 1990s.* London: Child Poverty Action Group.

Walther, A. (2006). "Regimes of Youth Transitions: Choice, Flexibility and Security in Young People's Experiences across Different European Contexts," *Young, Volume* 2, pp. 119–139.

Walther, A., Stauber, B., *et al.* (eds.) (2002). *Misleading Trajectories: Integration Policies for Young People in Europe?* Opladen: Leske+Budrich.

White, M. and Epston, D. (1990). *Therapeutic Means to Narrative Ends.* New York: Norton.

Williamson, H. (1997). "Status Zero Youth and the Class: Some Considerations," In *Youth, the 'Underclass' and Social Exclusion*, edited by R. MacDonald, pp. 70–82. London: Routledge.

Wong, V. (2004). "From Personal to Structural: Towards Critical Change in Youth Work Practice," *Youth Studies Australia, Volume 23 (3)*, pp. 10–16.

Wong, V. and Shiu, W. (2003). "At the Bottom of the Cabinet: Youth Unemployment and Social Exclusion in Hong Kong," In *Social Exclusion and Marginality in Chinese Societies*, edited by H. B. Ku and M. K. Lee, pp. 191–206. Hong Kong: Centre for Social Policy Studies, The Hong Kong Polytechnic University. (in Chinese)

Wong, V. and Ying, W. (2006). "Social Withdrawal of Young People in Hong Kong: A Social Exclusion Perspective," *Hong Kong Journal of Social Work, Volume 40 (1–2).*

Wyn, J. and White, R. (1997). *Rethinking Youth.* London: Sage.

RESTORATIVE JUSTICE APPROACH TO YOUTH-AT-RISK

9

Francis Wing-lin LEE

Near the end of this book, the editor wishes to introduce a different approach in working with youth-at-risk (YAR) which is unlike the rationales and practices of the traditional approaches in justice—rehabilitative and retributive. With declining faith in the retributive and rehabilitative approaches to crime (deviance) and punishment, the Restorative Justice (RJ) models for the criminal justice system, which are claimed to be reparative and reintegrative for the offenders, to have healing effects on the victims, and to allow community involvement, have gained popularity in the last decade. In many countries (such as the U.S., the U.K., New Zealand, and Australia), increasing use is being made of RJ in criminal justice, especially for young offenders. In fact it is believed that the RJ approach to crime (a kind of deviance) could also be applied to working with YAR who have not yet acquired the status of offenders.

Restorative Justice—The Conception

In the criminal justice system, this development of RJ is underpinned by a belief that it can help deliver key criminal justice objectives, such as meeting victims' needs and reducing reoffending. RJ in the criminal justice system is actualised by bringing the victims, offenders, family members of each, and other key stakeholders together to meet to construct an action plan for repairing the harm caused by the offence and reducing the chances of reoffending. The formats of this victim-offender mediation can be of several kinds (Sullivan and Tifft, 2006). RJ is influenced by the theory of reintegrative shaming proposed by John Braithwaite (1989), who argues that societies, which effectively shame criminal behaviour, but do this within a cultural context of respect for the offender and which follow shaming with gestures of reacceptance, have low crime rates. RJ's success is often attributed to its being an ideal forum for reintegrative shaming (Johnstone, 1999).

Unruly behaviour or deviance of juveniles has always been a main concern of many countries that have tried to find effective methods to tackle the problem. Under the retributive orientation, offenders (deviants) would be punished according to their "wrongness," such as imprisonment and capital punishment (Anderson, 1997; Hart, 1963). With the increased emphasis on human rights, retributive corrections have been de-emphasised. Allen and Latessa (1997) and van Ness (1996) have stated that rehabilitative measures for offenders (deviants) have been developed to provide them with specific and tailored-made treatments. Through rehabilitation, it is hoped that offenders (deviants) are provided with sufficient training and education for reintegrating into society. But with the declining faith in the retributive and rehabilitative approaches to crime and punishment, RJ models of criminal justice have been advocated as preferred alternatives (Bazemore, 1998; Johnstone, 2002, 2003 and 2004; Maxwell *et al.*, 2000; Morris and Young, 2000; Sullivan and Tifft, 2001).

RJ has been defined as a "process whereby the parties with a stake in a particular offence (unruly behaviour) come together to resolve collectively how to deal with the aftermath of the offence (unruly behaviour) and its implications for the future." (Marshall, 1996:37) Different practices or programmes have been employed to actualise the models, e.g. peacemaking, family group conferencing, sentencing circles, victim-offender reconciliation programmes, etc. (Braswell *et al.*, 2001; Carlson *et al.*, 1989; Galaway and Hudson, 1996; Maxwell and Morris, 2000; Sullivan and Tifft, 2001; Walgrave, 2001). It is believed that an ideal RJ measure for treating an offender (deviant) should have the input of the victim, offender (deviant), their family members, concerned stakeholders and the community. Diagrammatically, the conception of RJ is presented in the following figure (Figure 9.1).

Most countries that have adopted a RJ model have it focused on young offenders (Bazemore, 1996; Crawford and Newburn, 2003; Wong, 2001 and 2002). Although no direct explanation could be

Figure 9.1: Conception of Restorative Justice

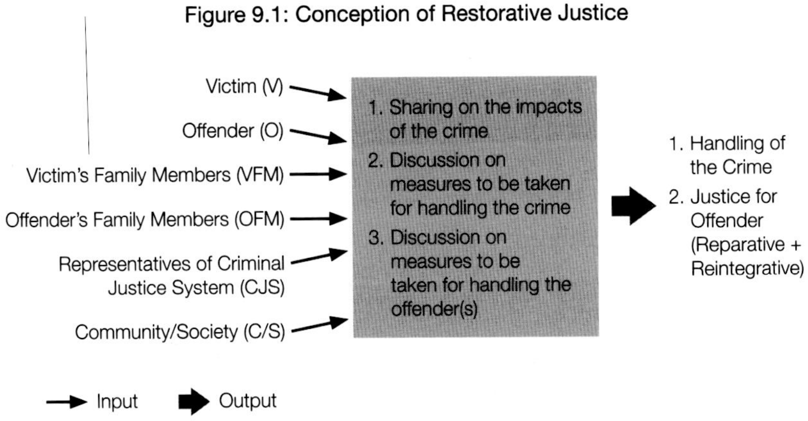

identified, it is conceived that young people (young offenders) are more able to change and be corrected (Lo *et al.*, 2005; Muncie, 1999; Omaji, 2003) and their committing of crime (deviance) is more unintended and impulsive, so RJ—more promising criminal justice alternatives—should be used on them.

A central conception in RJ is "shame." (Braithwaite, 1995; Miller and Blackler, 2000) It has been proposed that to treat the offender (deviant) with a "reintegrative shaming" orientation can help him to have remorse of his wrongdoing and prevent his re-commitment (Braithwaite, 1989).

Practice of RJ Approach with YAR in Hong Kong

Although the practice of RJ with YAR has not been formally or officially adopted in the social service system for young people in Hong Kong, experimentation of the workability of this approach and pilot implementation of related programmes have been attempted. It was with the faith of the effectiveness of employing the RJ approach to YAR of a group of school principals, social workers, and academics, that the Centre for Restoration of Human Relationships (www.restoration.com.hk) was established in August 2000 (Wong, 2005). With the endorsement of the Social Welfare Department, the Centre moved to its present location (a public housing estate) in 2003. In the meantime, most of the related programmes of the Centre, e.g. talks, workshops, life education projects, parents' training, and research and publications, are run in the school setting. Although no scientific and systematic evaluation has been carried out to see the effectiveness of this approach to unruly young people, with its gaining support and popularity, the perceived usefulness of this approach to YAR can be seen. Sharing with colleagues in the Centre has also indicated similar observations.

With the support of an academic from the City University, the use of this approach with YAR had been attempted from 1999 to 2003 in an outreach team of the Evangelical Lutheran Church of Hong Kong—Social Service (ELCHK). As the ELCHK started to operate a Community Support Service Scheme (CSSS) in 2005 that mainly works with cautioned young people, the RJ approach has been employed by this CSSS team since then. The main mediation method that the team employs for cautioned juveniles is Family Group Conferencing (FGC) (Ho and Chuk, 2005; Wan and Chuk, 2002). With the cooperation of Sheung Shui Police Station and Tin Shui Wai Police Station, cautioned juveniles—juveniles cautioned under the Police Superintendent's Discretion Scheme (PSDS)—are referred to the CSSS team for assessment of the suitability of mediation service.

Initially, the service was mainly for juveniles of minor property crime, such as theft in stores or from bicycles, etc. Later, it was extended to cover juveniles with individual conflicts. Parents of both parties—offender and victim—are also invited to the conference (meeting). As the cases have been under PSDS of the police, they also have representatives to attend the conferences. Their roles can be regarded as three: to witness the changes of the offended juveniles, to explain to the offended juveniles the process and significance of the PSDS, and to represent the community in encouraging and supporting the reintegration of the offended juveniles. The following is a case illustration of such a FGC.

Date:	December 2000
Venue:	Conference Room, Tin Shui Wai Police Station
Participants:	Ah Sze (Offender—YAR) and her mother, Ah Man (Victim) and his mother, School Social Worker, School Discipline Master, Police Officer (Police Inspector), and two Mediators—Mr. X and Ms. Y (from ELCHK CSSS).
Time:	14:00–15:30

The incident (offence):

Ah Man and his classmates met Ah Sze and her classmates in the playground after school. They were quarrelling because they had had a conflict a day before. During the quarrel, Ah Sze threatened to hit Ah Man, but Ah Man thought that she would not beat him and kept scolding. Then Ah Sze picked up a chair and hit Ah Man, while Ah Man tried to beat her back, too, but his classmates stopped him. A teacher passed by the scene and they all ran away. Ah Man was hurt on his head and bled, and then went to a nearby hospital, so the case was known to the Police and they investigated the incident. After the Police Superintendent in the concerned district considered the case, Ah Sze was cautioned under the Police Superintendent's Discretion Scheme. The Police referred the case to the CSSS of ELCHK. After the social workers of CSSS studied the case, it was decided that a mediation meeting, i.e. FGC, should be organised.

Brief process of the FGC:

When all participants were gathered in the Conference Room of the Police Station, the Conference began. Mr. X (one of the Mediators) invited the participants to introduce themselves, and then, after briefly recapitulating the incident, Mr. X further guided Ah Man (the Victim) to share the process of and his feelings towards the incident of being hit by Ah Sze (the

> *Offender). He was helped to ventilate his pent-up feelings and to deal with the negative emotions aroused by this incident. Ms. Y helped Ah Sze to visualise the unfavourable consequences of her behaviour, as Mr. X asked Ah Man to share how he was hurt in the incident. Ah Sze was guided by Ms. Y to recognise her misbehaviour and to send her apology to Ah Man. Then the Discipline Master (a teacher) of the School explained to Ah Sze and Ah Man the reasons why they had received punishment (one big demerit for each of them) from the School. The mothers of Ah Sze and Ah Man were both asked by Mr. X if they understood the reasons, and they indicated that they understood. They further admitted that, since they had to go to work, they did not give adequate supervision to their children. Then the Police Officer, who was present, was asked by Ms. Y to explain the process and significance of the cautioning. Finally, with the expressed support of the teacher, School Social Worker, and the parents, Ah Man accepted the apology of Ah Sze who was encouraged to tune back into the school life.*

Ah Man's (Victim's) feeling:

> *He said that he could understand more of the feeling of Ah Sze and why she had hit him in the incident. He was willing to accept her apology, and said that he would not take revenge on her.*

Ah Sze's (Offender's) feeling:

> *She said that she understood more about Ah Man's feeling in the incident and was really sorry for what she had done. She realised her wrongdoing and would try her best to control her emotions and would not hit anybody again.*

Although strictly speaking, the cautioned juveniles can be regarded as "offenders", in terms of the minor nature of their offences and mostly impulsive or unintended committing of the crime, they can be considered as YAR in an extreme view. Thus, this kind of victim-offender mediation service can be applied to these YAR for reintegration purposes. In the FGC, the victim's voice and feelings are heard, the reason(s) why the offender (YAR) did the act (unruly behaviour) is/are also shared, and support from family members of both parties can be solicited. It is believed that this FGC can help all parties to understand the situation more clearly. It can also meet victim's needs (voices being heard) and reduce reoffending by the offender (YAR), and most of all, it can help with the reintegration of the offender (YAR) back into the society. Sharing from colleagues who acted as mediators in the conferences further confirms the favourable result of this kind of mediation method.

Recommendations of RJ Practice for YAR in Hong Kong

A few years ago, in 2002, the Chief Justice's Working Party on Civil Justice Reform issued a consultation paper entitled *Civil Justice Reform: Interim Report and Consulting Paper*, seeking public opinion on the feasibility of civil mediation in Hong Kong. This was a sign saying that the time had come for Hong Kong to consider mediation services in legal issues. It has to be aware that if mediation services are to be adopted for YAR in Hong Kong, it signifies a change in the penal philosophy: from retributive and rehabilitative to restorative. If Hong Kong is to adopt the RJ approach in handling YAR or juvenile delinquents, several concerned governmental and non-governmental departments, such as the Social Welfare Department, Police Department, Correctional Services Department, NGOs with Youth Outreach Service, etc., have to establish mutual trust and close cooperation. It must be admitted that there are a lot of controversies concerning the adoption of the RJ approach for handling YAR in Hong Kong (Wong, 1996). The lack of clinical and local experience in running the FGC for referral purposes and the lack of resources, that is common for most social services in Hong Kong, are two limitations that have further handicapped the FGC attempts (Wan and Chuk, 2002). But if we put the benefit of young people to the forefront, believe in the unintendedness and impulsiveness of most of their committing of crimes, and agree with the philosophy of giving a chance to the juveniles, all the limitations are technical and solvable.

With reference to the situation in Hong Kong, the following are some recommendations of RJ practice for YAR in Hong Kong:

(a) FGC (with the involvement of family members) seems to be an ideal mediation format for RJ practice for YAR in Hong Kong.

(b) RJ approach (i.e. FGC) is more appropriately applied to juveniles who have committed offences of a minor nature (e.g. shop-theft, common assault).

(c) The FGCs should be further implemented with the cooperation of different district Youth Outreaching Teams (YOTs) and the respective district police stations.

(d) If RJ is to be used as an alternative approach to prosecution for YAR, it would be better if the FGCs are conducted for the juveniles (YAR) and no cautions will be performed, since the latter would have the records of the YAR filed in the respective police stations.

(e) Follow-up services and guidance for the victims and offenders (YAR) should be provided by the respective YOTs for the six months following, so as to offer assistance when needed.

References

Allen, H. E. and Latessa, E. J. (1997). *Corrections in the Community*. New York: Anderson Publishing Co.

Anderson, J. L. (1997). "Reciprocity as a Justification for Retributivism," *Criminal Justice Ethics,Volume 16 (1)*, pp. 13–26.

Bazemore, G. (1998). "Restorative Justice and Earned Redemption," *American Behavioral Scientist, Volume 41 (6)*, pp. 768–807.

Bazemore, G. (1996). "Three Paradigms for Juvenile Justice," In *Restorative Justice: International Perspectives*, edited by B. Galaway and J. Hudson, pp. 37–67. New York: Criminal Justice Press.

Braithwaite, J. (1989). *Crime, Shame, and Reintegration*. New York: Cambridge University Press.

Braithwaite, J. (1995). "Reintegrative Shaming, Republicanism and Policy," In *Crime and Public Policy—Putting Theory to Work*, edited by H. D. Barlow. New York: Westview Press.

Braswell, H., Fuller, J. and Lozoff, B. (2001). *Correctional, Peacemaking and Restorative Justice Transforming Individual and Institutions*. New York: Anderson Publishing Co.

Carlson, D., Crawford, T., van Ness, D. and Strong, R. (1989). *Restorative Justice Practice*. Washington, DC: Justice Fellowship.

Chen, X. (2002). "Social Control in China: Applications of the Labeling Theory and the Reintegrative Shaming Theory," *International Journal of Offender Therapy and Comparative Criminology, Volume 46 (1)*, pp. 45–63.

Crawford, A. and Newburn, T. (2003). *Youth Offending and Restorative Justice: Implementing Reform in Youth Justice*. London: Willan.

Galaway, B. and Hudson, J. (eds.) (1996). *Restorative Justice: International Perspectives*. New York: Criminal Justice Press.

Hart, H. L. A. (1963). *Punishment and Responsibility*. New York: Oxford University Press.

Ho, K. and Chuk, W. H. (2005). "Sharing of Professional Experience—Application of 'Restorative Justice'" in *Police Superintendent Discretion Scheme in Hong Kong*. (Paper presented in International Symposium of Criminal Justice Reform) (in Chinese) (19–20 August

2005) [Organised by Research Institute of Crime Prevention and Control, Nanjing University and Center for Restorative Justice, China University of Political Science and Law]

Johnstone, G. (1999). "Restorative Justice, Shame and Forgiveness," *Liverpool Law Review, (Special Issue): (Criminal Justice, edited by George Mair), Volume 21 (2/3)*, pp. 197–216.

Johnstone, G. (2002). *Restorative Justice: Ideas, Values, Debates*. London: Willan.

Johnstone, G. (ed.) (2003). *A Restorative Justice Reader: Texts, Sources and Context*. London: Willan.

Johnstone, G. (2004). "Informal and Restorative Justice," In *The Cavendish Handbook of Criminal Justice and Criminology*, edited by J. Muncie and D. Wilson. London: Cavendish.

Lo, T. W., Wong, D. and Maxwell, G. (2005). *Alternatives to Prosecution: Rehabilitative and Restorative Models of Youth Justice*. Singapore: Marshall Cavendish Academic.

Marshall, T. F. (1996). "The Evolution of Restorative Justice in Britain," *European Journal on Criminal Policy and Research, Volume 4 (4)*, pp. 21–43.

Maxwell G. and Morris, A., Eds. (2000). *Restorative Justice for Juveniles: Conferencing, Mediation and Circle*. New York: Hart Publishing.

Maxwell, G., Morris, A. and van Ness, D. (2000). "Introducing Restorative Justice," In *Restorative Justice for Juveniles: Conferencing, Mediation and Circle*, edited by G. Maxwell and A. Morris, pp. 3–16. New York: Hart Publishing.

Miller, S. and Blackler, J. (2000). "Restorative Justice: Retribution, Confession and Shame," In *Restorative Justice: Philosophy to Practice*, edited by Strang, H. and Braithwaite, J., pp. 77–91. Aldershot: Ashgate.

Morris, A. and Young, W. (2000). "Reforming Criminal Justice: The Potential of Restorative Justice," In *Restorative Justice: Philosophy to Practice*, edited by Strang, H. and Braithwaite, J., pp. 11–31. Aldershot: Ashgate.

Muncie, J. (1999). *Youth and Crime: A Critical Introduction*. London: SAGE.

Omaji, P. O. (2003). *Responding to Youth Crime: Towards Radical Criminal Justice Partnerships*. Sydney: Hawkins Press.

Sullivan, D. and Tifft, L. (2001). *Restorative Justice: Healing the Foundations of Our Everyday Lives*. New York: Willow Tree Press.

Sullivan, D. and Tifft, L. (eds.) (2006). *Handbook of Restorative Justice: A Global Perspective* London: Routledge.

van Ness, D. (1996). "Restorative Justice and International Human Right," In *Restorative Justice: International Perspectives,* edited by B. Galaway and J. Hudson, pp. 17–35. New York: Criminal Justice Press.

Walgrave, L. (ed.) (2001). *Repositioning Restorative Justice,* pp. 265–278. New York: William Publishing.

Wan, K. H. and Chuk, W. H. (2002). *Restorative Justice: A Way Forward in Hong Kong.* (Paper presented in International Conference on Offender Rehabilitation in the 21st Century) (2–5 December 2002) [Organised by the Society of Rehabilitation and Crime Prevention, Hong Kong (SRACP) and Chinas Prison Society]

Wong, D. S. W. (1996). *Shame and Reintegration: A New Approach of Working with Deviant Adolescents.* Hong Kong: Department of Applied Social Studies, CityUHK (in Chinese).

Wong, D. S. W. (2001). *Treating Delinquents with Restorative Justice in Hong Kong,* pp. 305–310. Conference Proceedings of the Regional Symposium of Juvenile Crime Prevention. Taipei: Central Police University (in Chinese).

Wong, D. S. W. (2002). *The Development of Restorative Justice for Juvenile Delinquents in Hong Kong.* Paper presented at the International Conference on Conferencing, Circles And Restorative Justice, Minneapolis, Minnesota US, 7–10 August 2002.

Wong, D. S. W. (March 2005). *Restorative Justice for Juveniles in Hong Kong: Reflections of a Practitioner.* (Plenary) Proceedings of the Sixth International Conference on Conferencing, Circles and Other Restorative Practices. Penrith, Australia: International Institute of Restorative Practices, pp. 71–85.

Zehr, H. (1997). "Restorative Justice: The Concept," *Correction Today, Volume 59 (7),* pp. 68–71. www.restoration.com.hk.